A Tiger by the Tail

A Tiger by the Tail

A 40-Years' Running Commentary
on Keynesianism by Hayek

With an essay on
'The Outlook for the 1970s:
Open or Repressed Inflation?'
by
F.A. HAYEK
Nobel Laureate 1974

Compiled and Introduced by
Sudha R. Shenoy

Introduction by
Joseph T. Salerno

Third Edition

Published jointly by
The Institute of Economic Affairs
and the
Ludwig von Mises Institute

Large Print Edition published 2013 by Skyler J. Collins.
Visit: www.skylerjcollins.com

First published by the Institute of Economic Affairs, London in 2009.
Visit: www.iea.org.uk

Third Edition 2009 © The Institute of Economic Affairs
New Material 2009 © Ludwig von Mises Institute, Creative Commons 3.0

All rights reserved. Written permission must be secured from the publisher to use or reproduce any part of this book, except for brief quotations in critical reviews or articles.

ISBN-13: 978-1494370008
ISBN-10: 149437000X

Acknowledgements

We are grateful to Routledge and Kegan Paul, the Editors of *The Economic Journal* and Professor Hayek for permission to reproduce extracts or articles.

— Editor

CONTENTS

Acknowledgements v
Guide to Extracts and Articles. xi
Introduction to the Third Edition by Joseph T. Salerno xiii
Preface by Arthur Seldon. xxi
Preface to the Second Edition by Arthur Seldon xxv
The Authors xxvii

I.   The Debate, 1931–1971: Sudha Shenoy 1
      Challenge to Keynes 2
      The Approach to an Incomes Policy. 5
      'Micro' Dimensions Acknowledged 9
      Is There a Price 'Level'? 10
      Further Implications of Hayekian Analysis. 13

II.   The Misuse of Aggregates. 15
    1. Inflationism 15
    2. No Causal Connection Between Macro Totals and
       Micro Decisions 16
    3. Fallacy of 'The' Price Level 17
    4. Economic Systems Overleap National Boundaries . . . 18
        Misleading Concepts of Prices and Incomes. 19
    5. Dangers of 'National' Stabilisation 20
        Theoretical Case Not Argued. 21
        Relative Price and Cost Structures 22
    6. Monetary Danger of Collective Bargaining. 24

III. Neglect of Real for Monetary Aspects 27
7. Keynes's Neglect of Scarcity 27
Investment Demand and Incomes 28
Final Position of Rate of Return. 29
Mr. Keynes's Economics of Abundance 30
Basic Importance of Scarcity 33
8. Importance of Real Factors. 34
Significance of Rate of Saving 35
9. Dangers of the Short Run. 37
Betrayal of Economists' Duty. 39

IV. International versus National Policies 41
10. A Commodity Reserve Currency 41
An Irrational but Real Prestige. 42
11. Keynes's Comment on Hayek 43
Conditions for National Price Stability 44
Different National Policies Needed 45
12. F.D. Graham's Criticism of Keynes 47
The 'Natural Tendency of Wages' 48
Gold Standard 'Dictation' 50
Unanchored Medium of Exchange. 51
The Real Problem of Unemployment. 53
Professor Hayek's 'Intransigence' 54
13. Keynes's Reply to Graham 56

V. Wage Rigidities and Inflation 59
14. Full Employment, Planning and Inflation. 59
Full Employment the Main Priority. 60
Unemployment and Inadequate Demand. 61
Main Cause of Recurrent Unemployment 63
Expansion May Hinder Adjustment. 65

CONTENTS

15. Inflation Resulting from Downward Inflexibility of Wages 67
    - Importance of Relative Wages 68
    - Inflation—A Vicious Circle 70
    - The State of Public Opinion 72
16. Labour Unions and Employment 73
    - Changed Character of the Problem 74
    - Union Coercion of Fellow Workers 78
    - Wage Increases at Expense of Others 80
    - Harmful and Dangerous Activities 82
    - Acting against Members' Interests 84
    - A Non-coercive Role 87
    - Minor Changes in the Law 90
    - Responsibility for Unemployment 93
    - Progression to Central Control 96
    - 'Unassailable' Union Powers 99
17. (a) Inflation—A Short-term Expedient
    (b) Inflation—The Deceit is Short-lived 101
    - *17. (a) Inflation—A Short-term Expedient* 101
    - Inflation Similar to Drug-taking 102
    - Accelerating Inflation 104
  - The Path of Least Resistance 105
    - *17. (b) Inflation—The Deceit is Short-lived* 106
    - Limited Central Bank Influence 107
    - Weak Opposition to Inflation 108

VI. Main Themes Restated 111
  18. Personal Recollections of Keynes 111
    - Keynes Changes His Mind 112
    - Thinking in Aggregates 114
    - Full Employment Assumption 115
    - Wide Intellectual Interests 117
  19. General and Relative Wages 119

  Unpredictability and the Price System 120
  Wage Rigidities 122
  Importance of Relative Wages 123
 20. Caracas Conference Remarks 125

VII. The Outlook for the 1970s: Open or Repressed Inflation?: F.A. Hayek 127
  Long-run Vicious Circle 127
  Repressed Inflation a Special Evil 129
  Central Control and 'Politically Impossible' Changes 130
  Profit-sharing a Solution 132
  Basic Causes of Inflation 132

VIII. Addendum 1978 135
  Introduction by Sudha Shenoy 135
  Guiding Role of Individual Price Changes 136
 21. Good and Bad Unemployment Policies 138
  Maladjustments 139
  Wages and Mobility 140
  Dangers Ahead 141
 22. Full Employment Illusions 142
  Money Expenditure and Employment 143
  An Old Argument in New Form 144
  The Shortcomings of Fiscal Policy 145
  Cyclical Unemployment 146
  Consumers' Goods Demand and Investment Activity 148
  Purchasing Power and Prosperity 148
  Why the Slump in Capital Goods Industries? 148
 23. Full Employment in a Free Society 151

Hayek's Writings: A List for Economists 157
Index 159

Guide to Extracts and Articles
(Chapters II to VIII)

F. A. Hayek:

Prices and Production (1931)

Monetary Nationalism and International Stability (1937)

The Pure Theory of Capital (1941)

'A Commodity Reserve Currency', *Economic Journal* (1943)

Studies in Philosophy, Politics and Economics (1967)

The Constitution of Liberty (1960)

'Personal Recollections of Keynes and the "Keynesian Revolution",' *The Oriental Economist* (1966)

'Competition as a Discovery Procedure', *New Studies in Philosophy, Politics and Economics* (1978)

'Caracas Conference Remarks', Mont Pèlerin Conference (1969)

'Good and Bad Unemployment Policies', *Sunday Times* (1944)

'Full Employment Illusions', *Commercial & Financial Chronicle* (1946)

'Full Employment in a Free Society', *Fortune* (1945)

J. M. Keynes:

'The Objective of International Price Stability', *Economic Journal* (1943)

'Note by Lord Keynes', *Economic Journal* (1944)

F. D. Graham:
: 'Keynes vs. Hayek on a Commodity Reserve Currency', *Economic Journal* (1944)

Introduction to the Third Edition

The small book you are holding in your hands is unique. It is perhaps the finest introduction to the thought of a major thinker ever published in the discipline of economics. What makes it unique is the fact that it comprises selections and short excerpts from a broad range of Hayek's works written over a span of forty years. Despite its broad coverage the book is amazingly compact and coherent, seamlessly integrating the main themes from Hayek's writings on money, capital, business cycles, and international monetary systems. Furthermore, although it mainly uses Hayek's own words, some from his more technical works, it has been compiled and arranged by the late Sudha Shenoy in a way that makes it comprehensible to the layperson and student but can also be read with profit by the professional economist and teacher. Because of Shenoy's brilliant choice and arrangement of the twenty-three separate excerpts and her own illuminating, but never intrusive, introductions to each separate selection, the book stands as a work in its own right and gives new insight into Hayek's thought. In a real sense, it is as much Shenoy's book as it is Hayek's.

The publication of the new edition of this classic could not have come at a better time, moreover. For it is not merely an outstanding contribution to intellectual history, but also a tract for *our* times. The U.S. has been mired in an officially-recognized recession for more than a year now with no end in sight. Our current downturn is fast becoming the lengthiest and most severe of the post-World War II era. Entering its fourteenth month, it has already surpassed the average length of the last six recessions and is rapidly approaching the postwar record of sixteen months. The net decline in employment of 2.6 million recorded for 2008 represents the greatest absolute decline in the number of jobs since 1945. With over a half-million workers losing their jobs in December 2008 alone, the unemployment rate unexpectedly spiked from 6.8 percent in November 2008 to 7.2 percent, the highest level in sixteen years. The 4.78 million Americans now claiming unemployment insurance is the highest since 1967, when this statistic began to be recorded and represents the highest proportion of the work force since 1983. Adding to the dismal employment picture, the average work week for the month plummeted to 33.3 hours, the lowest level since 1964, while part-time jobs shot up by 700,000, or nearly 10 percent, from the previous month, indicating that many part-time workers counted as officially employed were either previously terminated from full-time jobs or reduced from full-time to part-time employment by their current employers. Other indicators of the severity of recession besides employment reveal that the current recession has been deeper than the average recession, including industrial production, real income, and retail sales. As one Fed economist concluded, "Main recession indicators tend to support the claim that this recession could be the most severe in the past 40 years."[1]

Indeed the dread word "depression" is now being used by some economists and media pundits to portray our current difficulties, conjuring up the specter of the prolonged mass unemployment amidst idle industrial capacity and unsold piles of raw materials that marked the 1930s. For most recognized experts and opinion leaders, how we got into our current difficulties is now a moot question. Everyone is clamoring for a way out. A massive government bailout involving $700 billion to purchase risky assets and to subsidize troubled financial service and domestic automobile firms has proven spectacularly ineffective in reversing or even slowing the contraction of the economy,

---

[1] Charles Gascom, "The Current Recession: How Bad Is It?" Federal Reserve Bank of St. Louis Economic Synopses 4 (January 8, 2009): 2, available at *http://research.stlouisfed.org/publications/es/09/ES0904.pdf*.

although it has led to a staggering projected federal budget deficit of $1.2 trillion for the current fiscal year. Accompanying this deluge of red ink is highly inflationary growth in the official Fed monetary aggregates, with MZM shooting up by 10.1 percent and M2 by 7.6 percent year-over-year as of November 2008. Driving this monetary inflation has been the Fed's expansion of the adjusted monetary base by 76 percent over the same period, which has reduced the target Fed Funds rate from 5.25 percent in mid-2007 to less than .25 percent by the end of 2008.[2]

In response to the deepening economic crisis, politicians and their economic advisers are offering more of the same deficit-spending and money-creation snake oil. President Obama is promoting a massive $800-billion program of increased government spending and tax cuts over two years that includes the largest public works program since World War II. But this "stimulus program" is nothing but a continuation of the failed financial bailout under a new name. The Federal government will continue to spend and spend like a drunken sailor on shore leave. And, as Chairman Bernanke has indicated, the Fed will happily accommodate this orgy of wasteful and destructive spending by creating money to buy assets of every kind imaginable.

---

[2] It should be briefly noted that this was the same cheap money policy that ignited and stoked the unsustainable real estate boom in the first place. Thus from December 1999 through December 2005, the Fed increased the money supply as measured by MZM by about $2.5 trillion, or 57 percent, which works out to an uncompounded annual rate of 9.5 percent. During the same time period another Fed monetary aggregate, M2, registered an increase of $2 trillion, or about 44 percent, which yields an uncompounded annual rate of 7.3 percent. This massive monetary inflation was naturally accompanied by a precipitous decline in interest rates, with the target Fed Funds rate plunging from 6.5 percent in late 2000 to 1.0 percent in mid-2003 and being pegged at that level for nearly a year and then remaining below 3.0 percent for almost another year. Mortgages rates followed this sharp downward movement, with the rate on 30-year conventional fixed mortgages dropping 3 percentage points, from 8.52 percent in mid-2000 to 5.58 percent in mid-2005. But this understates the looseness in the home loan markets generated by the monetary inflation, which also induced the development of a remarkable laxity in credit standards. The statistics in this footnote and in the associated paragraph in the text are based on data from The Federal Reserve Bank of St. Louis Economic Research available at *http://research.stlouisfed.org/*).

Crude, old-style Keynesianism has thus returned with a vengeance. In truth, it never really left. Despite all the talk by government policymakers and central bankers and their macroeconomic advisers that they have painstakingly developed and learned to deploy sophisticated new tools of "stabilization policy" in the last twenty-five years, their tool shed is, in actual practice, completely bare of all but the blunt and well-worn instruments of deficit spending and cheap money. For their part, the mandarins of academic macroeconomics have revealed the total intellectual bankruptcy of their discipline and the laughable irrelevance of their formal models by abandoning all scholarly reserve and decorum and stridently promoting and endorsing the long discredited policies of old-fashioned Keynesianism. The amazing, knee-jerk resort to simplistic Keynesian remedies by the macroeconomics establishment in the current crisis is tantamount to the admission that there has been absolutely no progress in the postwar era in understanding the causes and cures of business cycles. This reveals a deeper and more chilling truth: contemporary stabilization policy is implicitly based on one of the oldest and most naïve of all economic fallacies, one that has been repeatedly demolished by sound economic thinkers since the mid-eighteenth century. This fallacy is that there exists a direct causal link between the total volume of money spending and the levels of total employment and real income.

In this book, Hayek provides an incisive critique of this fallacy in its Keynesian form and demonstrates the dire consequences of pursuing policies based on it. But the book contains much more than a critique of fallacious theories and policies: it holds the recipe for a solid and steady recovery from our current *depression* (and yes, always the straight-talker, Hayek uses this forbidden word).

In brief, Hayek argues that all depressions involve a pattern of resource allocation, including and especially labor, that does not correspond to the pattern of demand, particularly among higher-order industries (roughly, capital goods) and lower-order industries (roughly, consumer goods). This mismatch of labor and demand occurs during the prior inflationary boom and is the result of entrepreneurial errors induced by a distortion of the interest rate caused by monetary and bank credit expansion. More importantly, any attempt to cure the depression via deficit spending and cheap money, while it may work temporarily, intensifies the misallocation of resources relative to the demands for them and only postpones and prolongs the inevitable adjustment. The reason why this is not perceived by Keynesians is because of an implicit assumption that Hayek identified in Keynes's writings. Keynes wrongly assumed that unemployment typically involves the idleness of resources of all kinds in all stages of production. In this sense Keynesian economics left out the vital element of the scarcity of real resources, the *pons asinorum* of undergraduate economic principles courses. In Keynes's illusory world of superabundance, an increase in total money expenditure will indeed increase employment and real income, because all the resources needed for any production process will be available in the correct proportions at current prices. However, in the real world of scarcity, as Hayek shows, unemployed resources will be of specific kinds and in specific industries, for example unionized labor in mining or steel fabrication. Under these circumstances, an increase in expenditure will increase employment, but only by raising overall prices and making it temporarily profitable to re-employ these idle resources by combining them with resources misdirected away from other industries where they were already employed. When costs of production have once again caught up with the rise in output prices, unemployment will once again appear, but this time in a more severe form because of the misallocation of additional resources. The government and central bank will then once again face the dilemma of allowing unemployment or expanding the stream of money spending. This sets up the conditions for an ever-accelerating monetary and price inflation punctuated by periods of worsening unemployment as was the case during the Great Inflation of the 1970s and early 1980s.

The alternative to this, Hayek argues, is to eschew monetary inflation and permit the prices of the unemployed resources to naturally readjust downward to levels that are sustainable at the current level of money income. In this case, unemployed labor and other resources will be guided by the price system into production processes that are sustainable at the current level of monetary expenditure. Permitting the market adjustment of relative prices and wage rates thus ensures a structure of resource employment that is coordinated with the structure of resource demands. In contrast, inflating aggregate money expenditure leads to a short-run increase in employment that causes an inappropriate distribution of resources whose inevitable correction ensures another depression. Such a correction can be postponed, but never obviated, only by repeatedly neutralizing relative price changes through accelerating inflation.

Those who deny Hayek's analysis—as all contemporary mainstream macroeconomists and policymakers do—and promote ever-increasing spending as the panacea for our present crisis live in the simplistic Keynesian fantasy land from which scarcity of real resources has been banished and in which the scarcity of money and credit is the only constraint on economic activity. As Hayek pointed out, such people do not merit the name "economist":

> I cannot help regarding the increasing concentration on short-run effects—which in this context amounts to the same thing as a concentration on purely monetary factors—not only as a serious and dangerous intellectual error, but as a betrayal of the main duty of the economist and a grave menace to our civilization. To the understanding of the forces which determine the day-to-day changes of business, the economist has probably little to contribute that the man of affairs does not know better. It used, however, to be regarded as the duty and the privilege of the economist to study and to stress the long-run effects which are apt to be hidden to the untrained eye, and to leave the concern about the more immediate effects to the

practical man, who in any event would see only the latter and nothing else.[3]

The recent bailouts and prospective stimulus package are aimed at reflating financial asset and real estate values back to levels inconsistent with the optimal distribution of labor and other resources as determined by the free interplay of market prices. And if enough money and spending are pumped into the economy, it is just possible that such a policy may, for a short while, freeze some resources in and return others to suboptimal employments, thus arresting or reversing our present downturn. But the advocates of these short-run spending palliatives are blind to what lies beyond: the long-run aftereffects of progressive inflation which, when eventually reined in, will result in an even more severe crisis and precipitous plunge into depression.

The prevailing macroeconomics paradigm has burst asunder along with the real estate bubble. Modern macroeconomists failed to forewarn against the dangers of the recklessly inflationary monetary policy pursued by the Fed in the first half of this decade. They now are at a complete loss for a coherent explanation of its consequences in the deepening financial crisis and recession that afflicts the global economy. Instead, they are reduced to reflexively prescribing the long obsolete Keynesian "stimulus" policy of deficit spending and cheap money—a sure recipe for a prolonged and grinding depression. Fortunately, there exists an analysis of business cycles—of bubbles, crises, and depressions—based on a long tradition of sound economic reasoning that will guide us out of the current morass to a steady and solid recovery. If one wishes to learn about this analysis, he or she can do no better than to start with a careful reading of *A Tiger by the Tail*.

— Joseph T. Salerno
January, 2009

---

[3] *The Pure Theory of Capital* (London: Routledge and Kegan Paul, 1953), p. 409; p. 29 in this volume.

Preface

The purpose of the *Hobart Paperbacks* is to discuss, in the spirit of what was once called 'political economy,'[4] the influences which affect the translation of economic ideas into practical policy and the economics of government activity. In the first *Paperback* Professor W.H. Hutt examined the notion that some ideas are not adopted because they are considered to be 'politically impossible.' In the second Mr. Samuel Brittan analysed the consistency of British Government economic policy since June 1970. In the third Mr. W.R. Lewis analysed the conflict between ideas and policy in the aspirations of the Treaty of Rome and the performance of its interpreters at Brussels.

The translation of economic thinking into government action is perhaps nowhere more vividly illustrated than in the work of John Maynard Keynes. He was the most influential economist of our times, his ideas have influenced governments of all philosophic flavours more than any other economist. Yet it is not clear that his work will survive longer than that of some of his contemporaries. Perhaps no economist more than Adam Smith has had both early influence on government policy and enduring influence on the thinking of economists of succeeding generations. The extent to which economic ideas are adopted by government does not necessarily reflect their contribution to fundamental economic truths. The reasons for their adoption may range from respect for the new insights they show on the working of the economy to cynical political expediency. If it is

---

[4]Professor T.W. Hutchison, *Markets and the Franchise,* Occasional Paper 10 (London: IEA, 1966).

true that a prophet is without honour in his own country it may be that the economists who most benefit mankind are without honour in their own times.

The powerful intellect of J.M. Keynes, his persuasive writing, and his capacity to formulate economic theory as specifics for government action not only made him the dominant economist, but also muted the doubts that some economists had about Keynes from *The General Theory of Employment, Interest and Money,* published in February 1936, and even earlier. Even though Keynes warned as early as 1945 of some of his followers who had gone 'sour and silly', and he seemed to be retreating in 1946 from his supposed demolition of the 'Classical' economic thought, his teachings have continued to dominate not only economic thinking in government but also economic teaching. G.D.H. Cole once wrote a book *What Marx Really Meant;* there may be debate for years to come on what Keynes really meant. Some economists never accepted the Keynesian system. They included not only A.C. Pigou, D.H. Robertson and others at Cambridge, but also the lesser-known but tenacious W.H. Hutt who, in his *Economists and the Public,* published seven months after *The General Theory,* warned against its inflationary implications, and in several other works that should be better-known than they are maintained that Keynes's analysis incorporated decisive defects.

The outstanding critic who was never persuaded by Keynes's analysis is F.A. Hayek, the Austrian scholar, who was teaching at the London School of Economics in 1936, and who has kept his British passport despite subsequent teaching posts in America, Germany and now in his native Austria.

Long before *The General Theory* Professor Hayek wrote a critique of Keynes's 1930 *Treatise on Money.* In the last 40 years he has written periodic criticisms of the Keynesian system, although at one stage he withdrew from the debate on monetary policy because he considered that Keynes, and the Keynesians, were not discussing the aspects that seemed to him fundamental.

Preface

The fourth *Hobart Paperback* comprises a series of 17 extracts from his writings and lectures, two from Keynes and one from F.D. Graham of Princeton University. They were assembled and are introduced by Miss Sudha Shenoy, an Indian economist who has studied and worked mainly in Britain. Together with a new essay written in July 1971 these extracts form an introduction to Professor Hayek's writings to which economists may wish to return, and which may induce others to consult for the first time.

Professor Hayek's writings prompt the reflection that the work of an economist should not be judged by the notice taken of him by politicians or even by other academics of his day. Why was Keynes so influential in his time and Hayek's (and other economists') reservations ignored? Why has Keynes dominated economic teaching for so long? How far is Keynesianism responsible for the acquiescence in post-war inflation? Are the doubts of many economists about Keynes now to be reflected in government thinking? Is taxation, as Keynes taught, still regarded as deflationary, or is it at last being seen that high tax rates and large deductions from earnings are inflationary? Has the Keynesian emphasis on macro-economics distracted attention from the structure of relative prices and costs that emerge from micro-economics?

This *Paperback* is offered as a contribution to the reconsideration of Keynesianism in the 1970s for teachers and students of economics, for policy-makers in government, for the civil servants who guide or misguide them, and for journalists who are sometimes more concerned with the fashionable than with the fundamental in economic thinking.

— Arthur Seldon
October, 1971

Preface to the Second Edition

The first edition of *Tiger by the Tail* made an almost immediate impact by reminding economists, the press and the public that for 40 years Professor Hayek's critique of Keynesian economics had been consistent, persistent and, in the end, vindicated. The extracts collated by Miss Sudha Shenoy comprised a graphic introduction to Professor Hayek's longer works since his early differences with Keynes.

The first edition was published in 1972 and was reprinted in 1973. Since the first edition the doubts about the Keynesian analysis, and its adaptation by economists who followed Keynes, have been increasing, and the readiness to listen to Professor Hayek's critique has accordingly grown. His work in general was, perhaps belatedly, recognised in the award of the Nobel Prize in 1974. And in 1975 *The Times,* which had not been Hayekian in the decades since the 1930s, paid Professor Hayek, in an oblique reference to *A Tiger by the Tail,* the tribute of identifying him as the economist above all who had accurately diagnosed the progression of inflation and its dangers to the economy:

> As Professor Friedrich Hayek has argued ever since his pre-war disputes with Keynes, the price of maintaining full employment by more and more inflationary public finance is not only accelerating inflation but also a progressive diversion of economic resources into activities favoured by or dependent on inflation. If inflation is to

be checked, that structural distortion has to be reversed, which must be painful.[5]

Nothing written by the neo-Keynesians has refuted this diagnosis; and it is now the common currency not only of an increasing number of economists but of economic commentators in the press in Britain, America and Europe.

As the continuing demand from readers for *A Tiger by the Tail* has occasioned a further reprinting, the original text has been made into a new edition by adding three pieces of writing in the mid-1940s in which Professor Hayek anticipated developments in economic affairs and policies 30 years and more later. As in the first edition, they are introduced by Miss Shenoy, who also writes on the significance for business decisions of the distinction between average and relative prices and on the secondary role of money supply.

The analysis is still relevant since governments in all countries that have allowed the tiger out of its cage are still pursuing its tail.

— Arthur Seldon
January, 1978

---

[5] *The Times,* 4 January, 1975.

THE AUTHORS

Friedrich August Hayek, Dr. Jur., Dr. *Sc.* Pol. (Vienna), D.Sc. (Econ.) (London), Visiting Professor at the University of Salzburg, Austria, 1970–74. Director of the Austrian Institute for Economic Research, 1927–31, and Lecturer in Economics at the University of Vienna, 1929–31. Tooke Professor of Economic Science and Statistics, University of London, 1931–50. Professor of Social and Moral Science, University of Chicago, 1950–62. Professor of Economics, University of Freiburg i.Brg., West Germany, 1962–68. He was awarded the Alfred Nobel Memorial Prize in Economic Sciences in 1974.

Professor Hayek's most important publications include *Prices and Production* (1931), *Monetary Theory and the Trade Cycle* (1933), *The Pure Theory of Capital* (1941), *The Road to Serfdom* (1944), *Individualism and Economic Order* (1948), *The Counter-Revolution of Science* (1952), and *The Constitution of Liberty* (1960). His latest works are a collection of his writings under the title *Studies in Philosophy, Politics and Economics* (1967) and *Law, Legislation and Liberty* (Vol. I: *Rules and Order,* 1973; Vol. II: *The Mirage of Social Justice,* 1976). He has also edited several books and has published articles in the *Economic Journal, Economica* and other journals. The IEA has published his *The Confusion of Language in Political Thought* (Occasional Paper 20, 1968), his Wincott Memorial Lecture, *Economic Freedom and Representative Government* (Occasional Paper 39, 1973), an essay in *Verdict on Rent Control* (IEA Readings No. 7, 1972), *Full Employment at Any Price?* (Occasional Paper 45, 1975), *Choice in Currency: A Way* to Stop Inflation (Occasional Paper 48, 1976), and *Denationalisation of Money* (Hobart Paper 70, 1976; 2nd edition 1978).

Sudha R. Shenoy, B.A., B.Sc.(Econ), M.A., was born in 1943 and educated at Mount Carmel School and St. Xavier's College, Ahmedabad, India, the London School of Economics, the University of Virginia, and the School of Oriental and African Studies, University of London. Formerly Research Assistant, Queen Elizabeth House, Oxford, 1971–73. Lecturer in Economics, University of Newcastle, NSW, Australia, 1973–74. Lecturer in Economics, Cranfield Institute of Technology, 1975–76. Senior Tutor in Economics, University of Newcastle, NSW, since 1977.

Her publications include 'The Sources of Monopoly', *New Individualist Review* (Spring 1966); 'Pricing for Refuse Removal', in *Essays in the Theory and Practice of Pricing,* Readings in Political Economy 3 (London: IEA, 1967); 'A Note on Mr. Sandesara's Critique', *Indian Economic Journal* (April/June, 1967); *Under-development and Economic Growth,* Key Book 10 (London: Longmans for the IEA, 1970); 'The Movement of Human Capital', in *Economic Issues in Immigration,* Readings in Political Economy 5 (London: IEA, 1970); *India: Progress or Poverty?,* Research Monograph 27 (London: IEA, 1971); and (with G.P. O'Driscoll, Jr.) 'Inflation, Recession, Stagflation', in E.G. Dolan (ed.), *Foundations of Modern Austrian Economics* (Kansas City: Sheed and Ward, 1976).

I. The Debate, 1931–1971*

By Sudha Shenoy

The roots of current economic ideas and of those guiding wages policy lie in the 1930s, in discussion inspired by the publication of the *General Theory*. Though Keynes's ideas diverged significantly from the theoretical structure of Pigou and Marshall, with which he was most familiar, 'Keynesian' ways of thinking had been fairly widespread in Britain and the USA before the *General Theory* appeared in 1936.[1] Keynes provided a theoretical foundation for these new ways of thinking.

Since the publication of the *General Theory* there has been an extensive elaboration of the theoretical system outlined in or generally associated with it, together with a further development of an alternative system of concepts called the Classical system. This was close to a mirror-image of the Keynesian system,[2] in the main relationships (e.g., between the quantity of money and total

---

*I should like to thank Dr. C.A. Blyth and Professors P.P. Streeten, L. Lachmann and I.M. Kirzner for reading this introductory essay and for their helpful comments. They do not necessarily share my interpretations.—S.R.S.

[1] Cf. Axel Leijonhufvud, *On Keynesian Economics and the Economics of Keynes* (Oxford: Oxford University Press, 1968); *Keynes and the Classics*, Occasional Paper 30 (London: IEA, 1969); T.W. Hutchison, *Economics and Economic Policy in Britain, 1946–66* (London: Allen and Unwin, 1968); H. Stein, *The Fiscal Revolution in America* (Chicago: University of Chicago Press, 1969).

[2] Cf. E.E. Hagen, 'The Classical Theory of Output and Employment', in M.G. Mueller (ed.), *Readings in Macroeconomics* (New York: Holt, Rinehart and Winston, 1966);

expenditure, between interest, saving and investment, between the wage level and the level of employment, and so on). But whereas the Keynesian system was couched wholly in terms of aggregates, the so-called 'Classical' system contained what may be termed a price dimension: the changes in the price 'level' associated with changes in the total money stock were held by the Classical system to imply equi-proportional changes in *all* prices, and variations in the price level in turn were associated with changes in the level of economic activity. In a sense the Keynesian approach may be regarded as a logical extension and elaboration of this rather crudely aggregative element in the 'Classical' system.

Challenge to Keynes
The doctrines generally accepted among English economists contemporaneous with Keynes were challenged, in fundamental respects, by an alternative analysis, developed on the Continent, and propounded in Britain by Professor Hayek. But by the 1940s, the Keynesian approach was almost universally adopted by economists. Initially, many appeared to believe that the 'macro' problems of unemployment and depression were solved and that few other major economic problems would emerge. The only problem remaining, it seemed, was the methods required to ensure 'full' employment.

> 'Now that the principle of adequate effective demand is so firmly established,' declared Professor Arthur Smithies, 'economists should devote particular attention to defining the responsibilities of the state.'[3]

H.G. Johnson, 'Monetary Theory and Keynesian Economies' in *Money, Trade and Economic Growth* (London: Allen & Unwin, 1962); 'Introduction' in R.J. Ball and Peter Doyle (eds.), *Inflation* (Baltimore: Penguin Books, 1969).

[3] Professor A. Smithies, in the *American Economic Review* (June 1945): 367. The symposium on employment policy, *American Economic Review* (May 1946), is also relevant.

The British White Paper on Employment Policy in 1944 and the full employment commitment in the UN Charter reflected this belief, as did the 1946 Employment Act in the USA.[4]

A few dissenting voices warned of trouble ahead. Professor Jacob Viner observed of a report to the Economic and Social Council of the United Nations, *National and International Measures for Full Employment,* prepared by a group of distinguished economists (J.M. Clark, A. Smithies, N. Kaldor, P. Uri and E.R. Walker):

> The sixty-four dollar question with respect to the relations between unemployment and full employment policy is what to do if a policy to guarantee full employment leads to chronic upward pressure on money wages through the operation of collective bargaining. The authors take a good look at the question—and run away.

Effective demand to provide employment was the 'key concept' in recommendations which Professor Viner rated as 'much more Keynesian than was the final Keynes himself...'[5]

---

[4]The Congress declared it was

> ... the continuing policy and responsibility of the Federal Government to use all practicable means ... to coordinate and utilize all its plans, functions and resources for the purpose of creating and maintaining ... conditions under which there will be afforded useful employment for those able, willing and seeking work.... (Quoted in Robert Lekachman, *The Age of Keynes* [London: Allen Lane The Penguin Press, 1967], p. 144)

[5]'Full Employment at Whatever Cost?', *Quarterly Journal of Economics* (August 1950). Earlier Professor Viner said:

> ... it is a matter of serious concern whether under modern conditions, even in a socialist country if it adheres to democratic political procedures, employment can always be maintained at a high level without recourse to inflation, overt or disguised, or if maintained whether it will not itself induce an inflationary wage spiral through the operation of collective bargaining ...

Shortly after the *General Theory* appeared, Professor W.H. Hutt argued that it was a specific for inflation.[6]

Even Keynes had doubts, a few years after the *General Theory*. In his essay *How to Pay for the War* (London: Macmillan, 1940) he warned the trade unions of the 'futility' of demanding an increase in money rates of wages to compensate for every increase in the cost of living. To prevent inflation, he insisted,

> Some means must be found for withdrawing purchasing power from the market; or prices must rise until the available goods are selling at figures which absorb the increased quantity of expenditure—in other words the method of inflation.

And in a discussion of financing war expenditure:

> ... a demand on the part of the trade unions for an increase in money rates of wages to compensate for every increase in his cost of living is futile, and greatly to the disadvantage of the working class. Like the dog in the fable, they lose

---

Reviewing the *General Theory* in *Quarterly Journal of Economics,* 1936–37, he said:

> In a world organised in accordance with Keynes's specifications, there would be a constant race between the printing press and the business agents of the trade unions with the problem of unemployment largely solved if the printing press could maintain a constant lead ...

[6]*Economists and the Public* (London: Jonathan Cape, 1936). Professor Hutt published a brief analysis of the central issues in his *Theory of Idle Resources* (London: Jonathan Cape, 1939); his earlier work on the *Theory of Collective Bargaining* (1930; new edition, Glencoe, Ill.: The Free Press, 1954; 2nd British edition published as *The Theory of Collective Bargaining 1930–1975,* Hobart Paperback No. 8 [London: IEA, 1975]) analysed the position of the Classical economists on the relation between unions and wage determination.

There is also a collection of extracts from reviews and other early writings critical of the *General Theory,* edited by Henry Hazlitt: *The Critics of Keynesian Economics* (Princeton, N.J.: D. Van Nostrand, 1960).

the substance in grasping at the shadow. It is true that the better organised might benefit at the expense of other consumers. But except as an effort at group selfishness, as a means of hustling someone else out of the queue, it is a mug's game . . .

The Approach to an Incomes Policy

Over the following 25-odd years, the early Keynesian theory was further elaborated and refined and a highly sophisticated series of macro-economic models developed. The 1950s more especially saw the discovery of 'cost inflation', in which a rise in wages pushed up the cost level. As prices were determined by costs, and, in crucial sectors of the economy, were 'administered' on the cost-plus-mark-up practice, prices rose to protect profit margins. But since wages were also incomes the cost and price increases had no deflationary effect, as effective demand rose simultaneously.[7] In these circumstances a contractionary monetary/fiscal policy would be deflationary: it would lead to socially intolerable levels of unemployment and excess capacity; an alternative measure, directed specifically at rising costs, would have to be devised. If price stability and full employment could both be achieved by keeping wage increases within the limits set by rises in productivity, this implied an 'incomes policy'. Further investigation into the implications for the price- and wage-level of linking sectoral wage increases with productivity strengthened the case for a nationally-determined 'wages policy' covering both relative wage-rates *and* the general wage level. If wages rose in the sectors where productivity was rising, the result would be a rise in demand for the outputs of other sectors, resulting in a rise in their prices.[8]

Economic policy in the UK and the USA, from 1950 on, reflected the adoption of these views; there was a gradual shift

---

[7] F. Machlup, 'Another view of cost push and demand pull inflation', *Review of Economics and Statistics* (1960).
[8] P.P. Streeten, 'Wages, prices and productivity', *Kyklos* (1962).

from exhortations, guidelines and pay pauses to more direct attempts to influence and control wages.[9]

That such direct control of wages and prices would be needed to forestall the 'vicious wage-price spiral'[10] resulting from full employment had been forecast by Lord Beveridge as early as 1944.

By the late 1960s and early 1970s more economists came to favour an incomes policy, some reluctantly (Robbins, Meade, Paish, Brittan, Morgan),[11] others enthusiastically (Balogh, Streeten, Opie).[12]

Lord Robbins's case is particularly interesting. In the early 1950s he analysed clearly the inflationary implications of the full employment policy contemplated by Beveridge: it gave union leaders a virtual guarantee that

> whatever [wage] rates they succeeded in getting, unemployment would not be permitted to emerge.[13]

It would give them a continuous incentive to push wages beyond increases in productivity, setting off a 'vicious spiral' of 'more inflation'. This, in turn, might force governments to act directly on wage rates.

---

[9] D.J. Robertson, 'Guideposts and Norms: Contrasts in US and UK Wage Policy', *Three Banks Review* (December 1966); D.C. Smith, 'Income Policy', in R.E. Caves and Associates (eds.), *Britain's Economic Prospects* (London: Allen & Unwin, 1968).

[10] W.H. Beveridge, *Full Employment in a Free Society* (London: Allen and Unwin, 1944, pp. 198–201, esp. p. 201: 'Adoption by the State of a price policy is a natural and probably an inevitable consequence of a full employment policy'.

[11] Lord Robbins, 'Inflation: The Position Now', *Financial Times,* 23 June, 1971; J.E. Meade, *Wages and Prices in a Mixed Economy,* Occasional Paper 35 (London: IEA for Wincott Foundation, 1971); F.W. Paish, *Rise and Fall of Incomes Policy,* Hobart Paper 47 (London: IEA, second edition, 1971); S. Brittan, *Government and the Market Economy,* Hobart Paperback 2 (London: IEA, 1971); E. Victor Morgan, 'Is Inflation Inevitable?', *Economic Journal* (March 1966).

[12] T. Balogh, *Labour and Inflation,* Fabian Tract 403 (Fabian Society, 1970); Streeten, 'Wages, prices and productivity'; R.G. Opie, 'Inflation' in P.D. Henderson (ed.), *Economic Growth in Britain* (London: Weidenfeld & Nicolson, 1966).

[13] Robbins, 'Full Employment as an Objective', in *The Economist in the Twentieth Century* (London: Macmillan, 1954); italics in original.

> The present determination of wages by bargain between employer and employed would be suspended. Wage-fixing by the state would take its place.

He believed, however, that this alternative would be rejected 'on the ground that in the end its efficient operation would prove to be incompatible with the continuation of political democracy. . . .'[14] Seventeen years later he argued[15] for an incomes policy as temporary *'shocktactics'*, to afford a 'breathing space' in which fundamental monetary-fiscal reforms might be 'advanced and understood'.

Despairing of the good sense of union leaders, he sought to bring pressure on them indirectly, suggesting that businessmen be restrained from granting inflationary wage increases by restrictions on aggregate demand, even to the point of precipitating bankruptcies, thus preventing the payment of higher wages that would simply be recouped by higher prices. A suggested alternative or parallel measure would be to tax inflationary wage increases granted by firms. He hoped that union leaders' expectations of automatic increases in wages would thereby be frustrated. (A similar view is taken by Professors E. Victor Morgan, F.W. Paish, and Sidney Weintraub.)[16]

An alternative type of incomes policy was proposed by Mr. Samuel Brittan.[17] The government would control the level to which wage rates would be permitted to rise while allowing employers short of labour to offer higher rates, but *without* pretending to determine relative wage rates on the basis of social justice. Such a policy, he said, must be treated as a *supplement* to monetary and fiscal policies that

---

[14] Robbins, 'Inflation', pp. 35–36.

[15] *Financial Times*, 23 June, 1971.

[16] Morgan, 'Is Inflation Inevitable', p. 14; Paish, *Rise and Fall of Incomes Policy*, Postscript; S. Weintraub, 'An Incomes Policy to Stop Inflation', *Lloyds Bank Review* (January 1971).

[17] Brittan, *Government and the Market Economy*, pp. 48–56.

provide sufficient demand to prevent unemployment, but prevent the emergence of excess demand. He suggested as a stop-gap a temporary price and wage freeze until these policies are implemented.

Two possible implications of this suggestion may be considered. First, if such a brake on wage increases is to be more than advice, unions must be willing to accept the guidance of the incomes authority—implying a permanent watchdog role for the authority (or at least an existence parallel to that of the unions-as-wage-fixers). If the unions refuse to cooperate presumably the authority will have to take over their wage-fixing function . . .

Secondly, in common with other recommendations for incomes policies, this proposal would perpetuate a given structure of *relative* wage rates since *all* the rates to which it applied would be allowed to rise only by a given percentage (save in 'labour scarcity'). This relative wage structure today reflects not so much the allocative forces of the market[18] but the relative power or 'pushfulness' of the different unions. Can we assume that they would be content to retain indefinitely whatever relative positions they had achieved at the moment the incomes policy came into existence?

---

[18]Professor W.B. Reddaway ('Wage Flexibility and the Distribution of Labour', *Lloyds Bank Review* [April 1959]) has suggested, on empirical investigations, that relative wage-rate movements have little allocative significance today: labour reallocation among industries and firms is achieved by changes in job offers. Given union-determined wage-rate structure, this is perhaps to be expected; but it is not incompatible with the basic proposition that prices are *capable* of performing allocative functions—*if* the institutional framework is designed to this end.

Professor Reddaway has argued elsewhere ('Rising Prices Forever?', *Lloyds Bank Review* [July 1966]) that rising prices are here to stay indefinitely. While advocating institutional restraints on price and wage increases, he recommends measures to raise productivity, arguing that, given such 'assured' increases in real income, even fairly high rates of price increase may be tolerated—the few hyperinflations in history being special cases. To live with inflations of the Latin American type, as he seems to contemplate (p. 15), would imply not only very substantial changes in British economic institutions (which he might have made explicit); it would also imply the acquiescence or political impotence of groups whose incomes remained static or failed to rise as fast as prices.

'Micro' Dimensions Acknowledged

The common thread running through these discussions is the alleviation of specific *wage-rate* maladjustments. They have moved some distance from the aggregative analysis. The 'macro' problem of adequate demand management has, it now appears, a 'micro' dimension: that of establishing (or obtaining) an 'appropriate' scale of prices. In other words, from the viewpoint of practical policy, the 'macro' problem of a persistent upward push (or pull) on the price 'level' is now seen to have 'micro' roots, in the specific 'pricing' methods used by specific groups of workers. 'Macro' measures acting on aggregate expenditure may have allowed us hitherto to ignore this basic micro *dis*coordination,[19] but events seemingly have brought the issue forward unavoidably. 'Macro' measures, it would appear, may *offset* micro problems but are no substitute for appropriate micro solutions.

The significance of coordination at the micro-level appears here, in the light of a third type of analysis, which Professor Hayek developed, on foundations laid by the 'Austrians': Menger, Wieser and Böhm-Bawerk, culminating in the works of Mises. Hayek concentrated on an analysis of the structure of relative prices and their interrelations. He did not adopt the framework of a general equilibrium system, nor treat price changes as elements in a 'dynamic' shift between two general equilibria. He regarded prices rather as empirical reflectors of specific circumstances and price changes as an *interrelated* series of changes in these 'signals', which produced a gradual adaptation in the entire price structure (and hence in the outputs of different commodities and services) to the constant, unpredictable changes in the real world. Pricing, in short, is seen as a continuous information-collecting and disseminating process, but it is the institutional framework that determines both the extent to which, and the degree of success with which, prices are enabled to perform this potential signalling or allocative function.

---

[19] Suggestions that wage increases be linked to productivity are clearly attempts to offer some *coordinative* criterion, in this discoordinated situation.

This 'Austrian' analysis constitutes a substantial break with Classical economic theory from Adam Smith to J.S. Mill. It differs also both from the doctrines of the English economists after Mill and from the theoretical preoccupations of the Lausanne School with the conditions of general equilibrium.[20]

Is There a Price 'Level'?
In his first English work, the four lectures published as *Prices and Production*,[21] Hayek questioned the concept of a price 'level'—i.e., a relationship between the total money stock and the total volume of production, variations in this 'level' being associated with variations in aggregate output. He argued that such a concept failed to show that there were specific influences of changes in the stream of money expenditure on the structure of relative prices, and hence on the structure of production.[22] These price and output changes, he maintained, occurred irrespective of changes in the price level. Hayek's analysis implied that if 'the' price 'level' is held 'stable' by offsetting monetary measures, under conditions where the relative price changes would result in a falling price 'level', the real dislocations would be the same as if prices were made to rise by monetary measures, if otherwise they might have remained 'stable.' In either case, the outcome is a painful correction of the preceding real misdirection, i.e., a 'depression'.

---

[20] F.A. Hayek, 'Economics and Knowledge', 'The Use of Knowledge in Society' and the three chapters on 'Socialist Calculation' in *Individualism and Economic Order* (London: Routledge, 1948).

[21] Routledge and Kegan Paul, 1931 and 1933. A scheme which confines itself to contrasting 'the "Classical" model' (i.e., the conceptual framework used by the English economists contemporary with Keynes) and 'the Keynesian (and/or post-Keynesian) model' may therefore be incomplete. H.G. Johnson, 'Monetary Theory and Keynesian Economies'; 'Introduction', in Ball and Doyle (eds.); and the 'Introduction' to R.W. Clower (ed.), *Monetary Theory* (Harmondsworth, U.K.: Penguin Books, 1969) are instances of such schemes.

[22] Professor Clower's stricture that 'at no stage in pre-Keynesian economics was any serious attempt made to build peculiarly monetary assumptions into the microfoundations of economic analysis' (*Monetary Theory*, p. 19) is not accurate.

During the 1920s, the widespread theoretical and policy influence of the 'stabilisationists' meant that considerations of the kind sketched by Professor Hayek were not incorporated into either theoretical or policy analysis; consequently, the price 'level' 'stability' of the period was read as implying a lack of maladjustment in the underlying price structure. (This is an extremely oversimplified summary of a complex historical situation, the specific conditions of which were not uniform in all countries.)

Theoretically and practically, it may be argued that in conditions of 'depression' there is little choice save to augment the level of monetary expenditure to the highest possible degree. Hayekian analysis, while readily conceding that depressionary symptoms may thus be overlaid, would argue that the problems are then transformed into those arising out of a situation where every reappearance of recessionary symptoms has to be met by ever larger increases of monetary expenditure, eventually issuing in the 'stag-flationist' dilemma.

This is not necessarily to say that the specific policies pursued in the 1920s and 1930s, or the economic and monetary framework of the time, represented an approximation to the Hayekian ideal. Hayek has said with regard to the period 1927–32:

> . . . up to 1927, I should, indeed, have expected that because, during the preceding boom period, prices did not rise—but rather tended to fall—the subsequent depression would be very mild. But, as is well known, in that year an entirely unprecedented action was taken by the American monetary authorities, which makes it impossible to compare the effects of the boom on the subsequent depression with any previous experience. The authorities succeeded by means of an easy money policy, inaugurated as soon as the symptoms of an impending reaction were noticed, in prolonging the boom for two years beyond what would otherwise have been its natural end. And when the crisis finally occurred, for almost two more years deliberate attempts were made

to prevent, by all conceivable means, the normal process of liquidation. It seems to me that these facts have had a far greater influence on the character of the depression than the developments up to 1927, which, from all we know, might instead have led to a comparatively mild depression in and after 1927.[23]

Shortly after the publication of the first edition of *Prices and Production,* Professor Hayek published (in *Economica*) the first part of a long, substantive review of Keynes's *Treatise on Money*.[24] This provoked a reply from Keynes, followed by a rejoinder, before the publication of the second part of the review. Hayek criticised Keynes for his neglect of the real structure of production, arguing that Keynes's predilection for concentrating on the immediate and purely monetary phenomena accompanying changes in money expenditure, together with his penchant for aggregative macro concepts (*total* profits, *total* investment), had led him into contradictory or untenable conclusions. Keynes apparently held that if there were no entrepreneurial profits or losses in the aggregate, total output would be held constant. Hayek replied that if profits in the 'lower' stages of production (nearer consumption) were exactly counterbalanced by losses in the 'higher' stages, there would be a contraction in the capital structure and a fall in output and employment—even though there were no aggregate profits or losses.

In his reply, Keynes failed to take up the numerous substantial criticisms made by Hayek. The main point of interest is his explicit statement that '. . . in my view, saving and investment . . . can get out of gear . . . there being no automatic mechanism in the economic system . . . to keep the two rates equal'. Hayek's reply to this was based on his analysis of the relative price-structure:

---

[23] *Prices and Production* (London: Routledge, 2nd ed., 1935), pp. 161–62.
[24] 'Reflections on the Pure Theory of Money of Mr. J.M. Keynes', *Economica* (August 1931 and February 1932); J.M. Keynes, 'The Pure Theory of Money—A Reply to Dr. Hayek'; F.A. Hayek, 'A Rejoinder to Mr. Keynes', *Economica* (November 1931).

> Mr. Keynes's assertion that there is no automatic mechanism in the economic system to keep the rate of saving and the rate of investing equal . . . might with equal justification be extended to the more general contention that there is no automatic mechanism in the economic system to adapt production to any other shift in demand.

Further Implications of Hayekian Analysis
There are further implications of the Hayekian approach:
(a) If the current level of output and employment is made to depend on inflation, a slowing-down in the pace of inflation will produce recessionary symptoms. Moreover, as the economy becomes adjusted to a particular rate of inflation, the rate must itself be continuously increased if symptoms of a depression are to be avoided: to inflate is to have 'a tiger by the tail'.
(b) To limit price or wage-rate increases by an incomes policy is to freeze a particular set of price and wage-rate interrelationships while underlying circumstances of supply and demand are continually changing. This is like the 'stability' of a set of defective gauges perpetually pointing to the same set of readings. It reinforces other institutional factors preventing the specific changes in relative prices and wage rates necessary to the maintenance of 'full' employment. Or, to put this same point from a different angle, if 'full' employment is to be maintained at union-determined wage rates (which are inflexible downwards), *all other* prices and wage rates must be adjusted to them: other prices and wage rates must be set at, or reach, levels consistent with this objective. *Even if* union-determined wage rates were held down to a maximum percentage increase, it still *does not* follow that the *same* percentage increase, or a lesser increase, in all other prices and wage rates would suffice to achieve 'full'

employment. *This* is why it may be necessary for incomes to rise faster than output, even to secure that increase in output.[25]

(c) The major objection to an incomes policy approach is that it merely freezes a given array of prices and wage rates. It does nothing to bring about coordination or to introduce coordinative institutions into the labour sector. So long as the *dis*coordinative potential of such non-market institutions as unions is not tackled, the problem will recur again and again. There may be no substitute for a very painful reshaping of institutions or other means of bringing within the ambit of the pricing system wage rates made impervious to market forces.[26] The alternative is a *permanent* incomes policy: an all-round fixing of wage rates and prices, i.e., an effectively centrally-controlled economy (with all its problems), although we may, as it were, 'back into' this situation unintentionally. This is to say nothing about whether it is desirable politically.[27]

---

[25]Incomes policy advocates implicitly assume that 'full employment' relative price and wage interrelationships once established can be maintained indefinitely; their implicit 'model' is that of a rigid real structure of outputs and prices on which a varying monetary stream impinges (see esp. Meade, *Wages and Prices in a Mixed Economy,* pp. 11–12; Morgan, 'Monetary Theory and Keynesian Economies'; Brittan, *Government and the Market Economy.* Hayek has characterised such a mode of thinking as belonging essentially to the naïve early stages of economic thought (*Pure Theory of Capital,* pp. 409–10; also see *Economica* [August 1931]: 273).

But if prices and wages are inflexible downwards, the 'full employment' level of expenditure may itself continually shift upwards, since the appropriate price changes can only be made by continually 'jacking up' the entire structure.

[26]A similar view was put by Professors William Fellner and Friedrich Lutz in W. Fellner *et al., The Problem of Rising Prices* (Organisation of European Economic Cooperation, 1961).

[27]This stress on the labour side need *not* imply that established firms (in the Western economies or elsewhere) are *never* at present protected against actual or potential competition and against actual or potential losses, either by the institutional framework or by economic policy. The Hayekian approach implies that *no* incomes and assets—whether business or other—be protected against losses. (F.A. Hayek, "Free" Enterprise and Competitive Order' in *Individualism and Economic Order* [London: Routledge, 1949], and 'The Modern Corporation in a Democratic Society . . .' in *Studies in Philosophy, Politics and Economics* [London: Routledge, 1967]).

II. The Misuse of Aggregates

1. INFLATIONISM

In 1931 Professor Hayek believed that the naïve inflationist view—that every expansion of monetary expenditure produces expansion in output—had been superseded; but this view was revived in 1936 by the General Theory *which strengthened the 'subtler inflationism' against which he directed his attack.*

While the more naïve forms of inflationism are sufficiently discredited today not to do much harm in the near future, contemporary economic thought is so much permeated by an inflationism of a subtler kind that it is to be feared that for some time we shall still have to endure the consequences of a good deal of dangerous tampering with currency and credit. It is my belief that some even of those doctrines which are generally accepted in this field have no other basis than an uncritical application to the problems of society in general of the experience of the individual, that what he needs is more money.[1]

(Preface to first edition of *Prices and Production*)

---

[1] This theme is elaborated in item 18 below.

2. NO CAUSAL CONNECTION BETWEEN MACRO TOTALS AND MICRO DECISIONS

Professor Hayek emphasises the operational significance of individual specific price changes in the real world; he also emphasises the ex post *nature of such statistical constructs as averages and aggregates.*

. . . What I complain of is not only that [the quantity] theory in its various forms has unduly usurped the central place in monetary theory, but that the point of view from which it springs is a positive hindrance to further progress. Not the least harmful effect of this particular theory is the present isolation of the theory of money from the main body of general economic theory. For so long as we use different methods for the explanation of values as they are supposed to exist irrespective of any influence of money, and for the explanation of that influence of money on prices, it can never be otherwise. Yet we are doing nothing less than this if we try to establish *direct* causal connections between the *total* quantity of money, the *general level* of all prices and, perhaps, also the *total* amount of production. For none of these magnitudes *as such* ever exerts an influence on the decisions of individuals; yet it is on the assumption of a knowledge of the decisions of individuals that the main propositions of non-monetary economic theory are based. It is to this 'individualistic' method that we owe whatever understanding of economic phenomena we possess; that the modern 'subjective' theory has advanced beyond the classical school in its consistent use is probably its main advantage over their teaching.

If, therefore, monetary theory still attempts to establish causal relations between aggregates or general averages, this means that monetary theory lags behind the development of economics in general. In fact, neither aggregates nor averages do act upon one another, and it will never be possible to establish necessary connections of cause and effect between them as we can between individual phenomena, individual prices, etc. I would even go so far as to assert that, from the very nature of economic theory, averages can never form a link in its reasoning.

(Prices and Production, pp. 3–5)

3. FALLACY OF 'THE' PRICE LEVEL

Professor Hayek points out that the ex post *statistical construct of a price index, which we call 'the' price level, is not a representation of reality—in the sense in which, say, the 'observations' of the physical sciences are such a representation. (He also refers—in 1937—to the serious monetary consequences of an attempt to offset by monetary policy downward inflexibility of prices and/or wage-rates.)*

It is clear that in this case the argument for a national monetary system cannot rest on any peculiarities of the national money. It must rest, and indeed it does rest, on the assumption that there is a particularly close connection between the prices—and particularly the wages—within the country which causes them to move to a considerable degree up and down together compared with prices outside the country. This is frequently regarded as sufficient reason why, in order to avoid the necessity that the 'country as a whole' should have to raise or lower its prices, the quantity of money in the country should be so adjusted as to keep the 'general price level' within the country stable. I do not want to consider this argument yet. I shall later argue that it rests largely on an illusion, based on the accident that the statistical measures of price movements are usually constructed for countries as such; and that in so far as there are genuine difficulties connected with general downward adjustments of many prices, and particularly wages, the proposed remedy would be worse than the disease.

(*Monetary Nationalism and International Stability*, p. 7)

4. Economic Systems Overleap National Boundaries

In tracing through the effects of a change in demand that crosses an international political boundary Professor Hayek shows the series of interconnected *price and income changes it produces, emphasising the basic point that it is these interlinked changes in relative prices that constitute reality, rather than 'movements' in some statistical price-'level'.*

The important point in all this is that what wages and what prices will have to be altered in consequence of the initial change will depend on whether and to what extent the value of a particular factor or service, directly or indirectly, depends on the particular change in demand which has occurred, and not on whether it is inside or outside the same 'currency area'. We can see this more clearly if we picture the series of successive changes of money incomes, which will follow on the initial shift of demand, as single chains, neglecting for the moment the successive ramifications which will occur at every link. Such a chain may either very soon lead to the other country or first run through a great many links at home. But whether any particular individual in the country will be affected will depend whether he is a link in that particular chain, that is whether he has more or less immediately been serving the individuals whose income has first been affected, and not simply on whether he is in the same country or not. In fact this picture of the chain makes it clear that it is not impossible that most of the people who ultimately suffer a decrease of income in consequence of the initial transfer of demand from *A* to *B* may be in *B* and not in *A*. This is often overlooked because the whole process is presented as if the chain of effects came to an end as soon as payments between the two countries balance. In fact however each of the two chains—that started by the decrease of somebody's income in *A,* and that started by the increase of another person's income in *B*—may continue to run on for a long time after they have passed into the other country, and may have even a greater number of links in that country than in the one where they started. They will come to an end only when they meet, not only in the same country but in the same individual, so finally offsetting each other. This means that the number of reductions of individual incomes and prices (not their aggregate amount) which becomes necessary in consequence of a transfer of money from *A* to *B* may actually be greater in *B* than in *A*.

Misleading Concepts of Prices and Incomes
This picture is of course highly unrealistic because it leaves out of account the infinite ramifications to which each of these chains of effects will develop. But even so it should, I think, make it clear how superficial and misleading the kind of argument is which runs in terms of *the* prices and *the* incomes of the country, as if they would necessarily move in unison or even in the same direction. It will be prices and incomes of particular individuals and particular industries which will be affected and the effects will not be essentially different from those which will follow any shifts of demand between different industries or localities.

This whole question is of course the same as that which I discussed in my first lecture in connection with the problem of what constitutes one monetary system, namely the question of whether there exists a particularly close coherence between prices and incomes, and particularly wages, in any one country which tends to make them move as a whole relatively to the price structure outside. As I indicated then, I shall not be able to deal with it more completely until later on. But there are two points which, I think, will have become clear now and which are important for the understanding of the contrast between the working of the homogeneous international currency we are considering, and the mixed system to which I shall presently proceed.

In the first place it already appears very doubtful whether there is any sense in which the terms inflation and deflation can be appropriately applied to these interregional or international transfers of money. If, of course, we *define* inflation and deflation as changes in the quantity of money, or the price level, *within a particular territory,* then the term naturally applies. But it is by no means clear that the consequences which we can show will follow if the quantity of money in a closed system changes will also apply to such redistributions of money between areas. In particular there is no reason why the changes in the quantity of money within an area should bring about those merely temporary changes in relative prices which, in the case of a real inflation, lead to misdirections of production—misdirections because eventually the inherent mechanism of these inflations tends to reverse these changes in relative prices.

(*Monetary Nationalism and International Stability,* pp. 21–24)

5. Dangers of 'National' Stabilisation

This extract indicates the extent to which policies of national price-'level' 'stabilisation' may cumulatively produce international inflation. If prices in general are not permitted to fall in regions where a fall is necessitated by changes in circumstances, the only other method of securing such a relative decline is by a general rise in prices in all other *regions.*

Indeed, if we take a somewhat more realistic point of view, there can be little doubt what will happen. While, in the country where in consequence of the changes in international demand some prices will tend to fall the price level will be kept stable, it will certainly be allowed to rise in the country which has been benefited by the same shift in demand. It is not difficult to see what this implies if all countries in the world act on this principle. It means that prices would be stabilised only in that area where they tend to fall lowest relatively to the rest of the world, and that all further adjustments are brought about by proportionate increases of prices in all other countries. The possibilities of inflation which this offers if the world is split up into a sufficient number of very small separate currency areas seem indeed very considerable. And why, if this principle is once adopted, should it remain confined to average prices in particular national areas? Would it not be equally justified to argue that no price of any single commodity should ever be allowed to fall and that the quantity of money in the world should be so regulated that the price of that commodity which tends to fall lowest relatively to all others should be kept stable, and that the prices of all other commodities would be adjusted upwards in proportion? We only need to remember what happened, for instance, a few years ago to the price of rubber to see how such a policy would surpass the wishes of even the wildest inflationist. Perhaps this may be thought an extreme case. But, once the principle has been adopted, it is difficult to see how it could be confined to 'reasonable' limits, or indeed to say what 'reasonable' limits are.

But let us disregard the practical improbability that a policy of stabilisation will be followed in the countries where, with stable exchanges, the price level would rise, as well as in the countries where in this case it would have to fall. Let us assume that, in the countries which benefit from the increase of the demand, the prices of other goods are actually lowered to preserve stability of the national price level and that the opposite action will be taken in the countries from which demand has turned away. What is the justification and significance of such a policy of national stabilisation?

Theoretical Case Not Argued
Now it is difficult to find the theoretical case for national stabilisation anywhere explicitly argued. It is usually just taken for granted that any sort of policy which appears desirable in a closed system must be equally beneficial if applied to a national area. It may therefore be desirable, before we go on to examine its analytical justification, to trace the historical causes which have brought this view to prominence. There can be little doubt that its ascendancy is closely connected with

the peculiar difficulties of English monetary policy between 1925 and 1931. In the comparatively short space of the six years during which Great Britain was on a gold standard in the post-war period, it suffered from what is known as overvaluation of the pound. Against all the teaching of 'orthodox' economics—already a hundred years before Ricardo had expressly stated that he 'should never advise a government to restore a currency, which was depreciated 30 p.c., to par'[2]—in 1925 the British currency had been brought back to its former gold value. In consequence, to restore equilibrium, it was necessary to reduce *all* prices and costs in proportion as the value of the pound had been raised. This process, particularly because of the notorious difficulty of reducing money wages, proved to be very painful and prolonged. It deprived England of real participation in the boom which led up to the crisis of 1929, and, in the end, its results proved insufficient to secure the maintenance of the restored parity. But all this was not due to an initial shift in the conditions of demand or to any of the causes which may affect the condition of a particular country under stable exchanges. It was an *effect* of the change in the external value of the pound. It was not a case where with given exchange rates the national price or cost structure of a country as a whole had got out of equilibrium with the rest of the world, but rather that the change in the parities had suddenly upset the relations between all prices inside and outside the country.

Relative Price and Cost Structures
Nevertheless this experience has created among many British economists a curious prepossession with the relations between national price- and cost- and particularly wage-levels, as if there were any reason to expect that as a rule there would arise a necessity that the price and cost structure of one country as a whole should change

---

[2]In a letter to John Wheatley, dated 18 September, 1821, reprinted in *Letters of David Ricardo to Hutches Trower and Others*, edited by J. Bonar and J. Hollander (Oxford, 1899), p. 160.

relatively to that of other countries. And this tendency has received considerable support from the fashionable pseudo-quantitative economics of averages with its argument running in terms of national 'price levels', 'purchasing power parities', 'terms of trade', the 'Multiplier', and what not.

The purely accidental fact that these averages are generally computed for prices in a national area is regarded as evidence that in some sense all prices of a country could be said to move together relatively to prices in other countries.[3] This has strengthened the belief that there is some peculiar difficulty about the case where 'the' price level of a country had to be changed relatively to its given cost level and that such adjustment had better be avoided by manipulations of the rate of exchange.

Now let me add immediately that of course I do not want to deny that there may be cases where some change in conditions might make fairly extensive reductions of money wages necessary in a particular area if exchange rates are to be maintained, and that under present conditions such wage reductions are at best a very painful and long drawn out process. At any rate in the case of countries whose exports consist largely of one or a few raw materials a severe fall in the prices of these products might create such a situation. What I want to suggest, however, is that many of my English colleagues, because of the special experience of their country in recent times, have got the practical significance of this particular case altogether out of perspective: that they are mistaken in believing that by altering parities they

---

[3] The fact that the averages of (more or less arbitrarily selected) groups of prices move differently in different countries does of course in no way prove that there is any tendency of the price structure of a country to move as a whole relatively to prices in other countries. It would however be a highly interesting subject for statistical investigation, if a suitable technique could be devised, to see whether, and to what extent, such a tendency existed. Such an investigation would of course involve a comparison not only of some mean value of the price changes in different countries, but of the whole frequency distribution of relative price changes in terms of some common standard. And it should be supplemented by similar investigations of the relative movements of the price structure of different parts of the same country.

can overcome many of the chief difficulties created by the rigidity of wages and, in particular, that by their fascination with the relation between 'the' price level and 'the' cost level in a particular area they are apt to overlook the much more important consequences of inflation and deflation.[4]

(*Monetary Nationalism and International Stability*, pp. 42–46)

6. MONETARY DANGER OF COLLECTIVE BARGAINING

This extract is noteworthy for its prediction, in 1937, of the process of wage-inflation of the 1950s and 1960s.

While the whole idea of a monetary policy directed to adjust everything to a 'given' wage level appears to me misconceived on purely theoretical grounds, its consequences seem to me to be fantastic if we imagine it applied to the present world where this supposedly given wage level is at the same time the subject of political strife. It would mean that the whole mechanism of collective wage bargaining would in the future be used exclusively to raise wages, while any reduction—even if it were necessary only in one particular industry—would have to be brought about by monetary means. I doubt whether such a proposal could ever have been seriously entertained except in a country and in a period where labour has been for long on the defensive.[5] It is

---

[4] The propensity of economists in the Anglo-Saxon countries to argue exclusively in terms of national price and wage levels is probably mainly due to the great influence which the writings of Professor Irving Fisher have exercised in these countries. Another typical instance of the dangers of this approach is the well-known controversy about the reparations problem, where it was left to Professor Ohlin to point out against his English opponents that what mainly mattered was not so much effects on total price levels but rather the effects on the position of particular industries.

[5] It is interesting to note that those countries in Europe where up to 1929 wages had been rising relatively most rapidly were on the whole those most reluctant to experiment with exchange depreciation. The recent experience of France seems also to suggest

difficult to imagine how wage negotiations would be carried on if it became the recognised duty of the monetary authority to offset any unfavourable effect of a rise in wages on the competitive position of national industries on the world market. But of one thing we can probably be pretty certain: that the working class would not be slow to learn that an engineered rise of prices is no less a reduction of wages than a deliberate cut of money wages, and that in consequence the belief that it is easier to reduce by the roundabout method of depreciation the wages of all workers in a country than directly to reduce the money wages of those who are affected by a given change, will soon prove illusory.

(*Monetary Nationalism and International Stability*, pp. 52–53)

---

that a working class government may never be able to use exchange depreciation as an instrument to lower real wages.

III. Neglect of Real for Monetary Aspects

7. KEYNES'S NEGLECT OF SCARCITY

Professor Hayek argues here that the Keynesian system rests implicitly on a denial of the existence of real scarcities, since it assumes that aggregate real output automatically changes in the same direction as total monetary expenditure—in other words, that every increase in money incomes automatically calls forth a corresponding supply of consumer goods and *of investment goods.*

Somewhat more careful consideration is needed of what exactly we mean here when we speak of an increase in investment. Strictly speaking, if we start from an initial equilibrium position where the existence of unused resources[1] is excluded by definition, an increase or decrease of investment should always mean a transfer of input from the production of consumers' goods for a nearer date to the production of consumers' goods for a more distant date, or *vice versa*. But where we assume that this diversion of input from one kind of production to another is accompanied, and in part brought about, by changes in total money expenditure, we cannot at the same time assume that prices will remain unchanged. It is, however, neither necessary nor advisable to adhere for our present purposes to so rigid a type of equilibrium assumption. At any rate, so far as

---

[1] This means unused resources which could be had at the ruling market price. There will of course always be further reserves which will be offered only if prices rise.

concerns the impact effects of a rise in investment demand which we discussed in the last chapter, there is no reason why we should not assume that the additional input which is being invested has previously been unemployed, so that the increase in investment means a corresponding increase in the employment of all sorts of resources without any increase of prices and without a decrease in the production of consumers' goods. This assumption simply means that there are certain limited quantities of various resources available which have been offered but not bought at current prices, but which would be employed as soon as demand at existing prices rose. And since the amount of such resources will always be limited, the effect of making this assumption will be that we must distinguish between the effects which an increase of investments and income will have while there are unused resources of all kinds available and the effects which such an increase will have after the various resources become successively scarce and their prices begin to rise.

Investment Demand and Incomes
The initial change from which we started our discussion in the last chapter, an invention which gives rise to a new demand for capital, means that with given prices the margin between the cost of production and the price of the product produced with the new process will be higher than the ruling rate of profit, i.e., that the marginal rate of profit on the former volume of production will have risen. The first result of this, as we have seen, will be that investment will increase, the marginal rate of profit will fall, and the cash balances will decrease till the desire for holding the marginal units of the decreased cash balances is again just balanced by the higher profits which may be obtained by investing them. This new rate of profit will be somewhere between the old rate and the higher rate which would exist if investment had not increased. But since this additional investment has been financed by a release of money out of idle balances, incomes will have increased, and as a

consequence the demand for consumers' goods will also increase, although probably not to the full extent, as some of the additional income is likely to be saved.

If we assume that there are unused resources available not only in the form of factors of production but also in the form of consumers' goods in all stages of completion, and so long as this is the case, the increase in the demand for consumers' goods will for some time lead merely to an increase in sales without an increase of prices. Such an increase of the quantity of output which can be sold at given prices will have the effect of raising the investment demand further, or, more exactly, of shifting our returns curve to the right without changing its shape. The amount that it will appear profitable to borrow and invest at any given rate of interest will accordingly increase; and this in turn will mean that, though some more money will be released from idle balances, the rate of interest and the rate of profit will be raised further. And since this process will have raised incomes still further, it will be repeated: that is, every further increase in the demand for consumers' goods will lead to some further increase of investment and some further increase of the rate of profit. But at every stage of this process some part of the additional income will be saved, and as rates of interest rise, any given increase in final demand will lead to proportionally less investment. (Or, what is really the same phenomenon, only seen from a different angle, successive increases of investment demand will lead to the release of decreasing amounts of money from idle balances.) So the process will gradually slow down and finally come to a stop.

Final Position of Rate of Return
Where will the rate of interest be fixed in this final equilibrium? If we assume the quantity of money to have remained constant, it will evidently be above the rate which ruled before the initial change occurred and even above the somewhat higher impact rate which ruled immediately after the change occurred, since every revolution of the

process we have been considering will have raised it a little further. But under our present assumptions there is no reason why, even when this process comes to an end, the rate of interest need have risen to the full extent to which it would have risen in the beginning had the supply of investible funds been entirely inelastic. Thus, under the conditions we have considered, the release of money from idle balances (and the same would of course be true of an increase in the quantity of money) may keep the rate of profit and interest lastingly below the figure to which it would have risen without any such monetary change.

Let us be quite clear, however, about which of our assumptions this somewhat surprising result is due to. We have assumed that not only the supply of pure input but also the supply of final and intermediate products and of instruments of all kinds was infinitely elastic, so that every increase in demand could be satisfied without any increase of price, or, in other words, that the increase of investment (or we should rather say output) was possible without society in the aggregate or even any single individual having to reduce consumption in order to provide an income for the additional people now employed. Or, in other words, we have been considering an economic system in which not only the permanent resources but also all kinds of non-permanent resources, that is, all forms of capital, were not scarce. There is indeed no reason why the price of capital should rise if there are such unused reserves of capital available, there is even no reason why capital should have a price at all if it were abundant in all its forms. The existence of interest in such a world would indeed be due merely to the scarcity of money, although even money would not be scarce in any absolute sense; it would be scarce only relatively to given prices on which people were assumed to insist. By an appropriate adjustment of the quantity of money the rate of interest could, in such a system, be reduced to practically any level.

Mr. Keynes's Economics of Abundance
Now such a situation, in which abundant unused reserves of all kinds of resources, including all intermediate products, exist, may occasionally

prevail in the depths of a depression. But it is certainly not a normal position on which a theory claiming general applicability could be based. Yet it is some such world as this which is treated in Mr. Keynes's *General Theory of Employment, Interest and Money*, which in recent years has created so much stir and confusion among economists and even the wider public. Although the technocrats, and other believers in the unbounded productive capacity of our economic system, do not yet appear to have realised it, what he has given us is really that economics of abundance for which they have been clamouring so long. Or rather, he has given us a system of economics which is based on the assumption that no real scarcity exists, and that the only scarcity with which we need concern ourselves is the artificial scarcity created by the determination of people not to sell their services and products below certain arbitrarily fixed prices. These prices are in no way explained, but are simply assumed to remain at their historically given level, except at rare intervals when 'full employment' is approached and the different goods begin successively to become scarce and to rise in price.

Now if there is a well-established fact which dominates economic life, it is the incessant, even hourly, variation in the prices of most of the important raw materials and of the wholesale prices of nearly all foodstuffs. But the reader of Mr. Keynes's theory is left with the impression that these fluctuations of prices are entirely unmotivated and irrelevant, except towards the end of a boom, when the fact of scarcity is readmitted into the analysis, as an apparent exception, under the designation of 'bottlenecks'.[2] And not only

---

[2] I should have thought that the abandonment of the sharp distinction between the 'freely reproducible goods' and goods of absolute scarcity and the substitution for this distinction of the concept of varying degrees of scarcity (according to the increasing costs of reproduction) was one of the major advances of modern economics. But Mr. Keynes evidently wishes us to return to the older way of thinking. This at any rate seems to be what his use of the concept of 'bottlenecks' means; a concept which seems to me to belong essentially to a naïve early stage of economic thinking and the introduction of which into economic theory can hardly be regarded as an improvement.

are the factors which determine the relative prices of the various commodities systematically disregarded;[3] it is even explicitly argued that, apart from the purely monetary factors which are supposed to be the sole determinants of the rate of interest, the prices of the majority of goods would be indeterminate. Although this is expressly stated only for capital assets in the special narrow sense in which Mr. Keynes uses this term, that is, for durable goods and securities, the same reasoning would apply to all factors of production. In so far as 'assets' in general are concerned the whole argument of the *General Theory* rests on the assumption that their yield only is determined by real factors (i.e., that it is determined by the given prices of their products), and that their price can be determined only by capitalising this yield at a given rate of interest determined solely by monetary factors.[4] This argument, if it were correct, would clearly have to be extended to the prices of all factors of production the price of which is not arbitrarily fixed by monopolists, for their prices would have to be equal to the value of their contribution to the product less interest for the interval for which the factors remained invested.[5] That is, the difference between costs and prices would not be a source of the demand for capital but would be unilaterally determined by a rate of interest which was entirely dependent on monetary influences.

---

[3] It is characteristic that when at last, towards the end of his book, Mr. Keynes comes to discuss prices, the 'Theory of Price' is to him merely 'the analysis of the relations between changes in the quantity of money and changes in the price level' (*General Theory*, p. 296).

[4] Cf. *General Theory*, p. 137: 'We must ascertain the rate of interest from some other source and only then can we value the asset by "capitalising" its prospective yield'.

[5] The reason why Mr. Keynes does not draw this conclusion, and the general explanation of his peculiar attitude towards the problem of the determination of relative prices, is presumably that under the influence of the 'real cost' doctrine which to the present day plays such a large role in the Cambridge tradition, he assumes that the prices of all goods except the more durable ones are even in the short run determined by costs. But whatever one may think about the usefulness of a cost explanation of relative prices in equilibrium analysis, it should be clear that it is altogether useless in any discussion of problems of the short period.

Basic Importance of Scarcity

We need not follow this argument much further to see that it leads to contradictory conclusions. Even in the case we have considered before of an increase in the investment demand due to an invention, the mechanism which restores the equality between profits and interest would be inconceivable without an independent determinant of the prices of the factors of production, namely their scarcity. For, if the prices of the factors were directly dependent on the given rate of interest, no increase in profits could appear, and no expansion of investment would take place, since prices would be automatically marked to make the rate of profit equal to the given rate of interest. Or, if the initial prices were regarded as unchangeable and unlimited supplies of factors were assumed to be available at these prices, nothing could reduce the increased rate of profit to the level of the unchanged rate of interest. It is clear that, if we want to understand at all the mechanism which determines the relation between costs and prices, and therefore the rate of profit, it is to the relative scarcity of the various types of capital goods and of the other factors of production that we must direct our attention, for it is this scarcity which determines their prices. And although there may be, at most times, some goods an increase in demand for which may bring forth some increase in supply without an increase of their prices, it will on the whole be more useful and realistic to assume for the purposes of this investigation that most commodities are scarce, in the sense that any rise of demand will, *ceteris paribus*, lead to a rise in their prices. We must leave the consideration of the existence of unemployed resources of certain kinds to more specialised investigations of dynamic problems.

This critical excursion was unfortunately made necessary by the confusion which has reigned on this subject since the appearance of Mr. Keynes's *General Theory*.

(*The Pure Theory of Capital,* pp. 370–76)

8. Importance of Real Factors

The following passage is the concluding section of a long, intricate and very closely argued exposition of the influence of price changes on the relative profitability of investment in the different stages of production; it demonstrates that it is the relative scarcities of types of goods in relation to the monetary expenditure on them that ultimately determine these prices and price changes. The whole discussion presents a sharp contrast to the 'en bloc' thinking of the macro-approach.

We will conclude the present treatment by once more stressing the fact that, though in the short run monetary influences may delay the tendencies inherent in the real factors from working themselves out, and temporarily may even reverse these tendencies, it will in the end be the scarcity of real resources relative to demand which will decide what kind of investment, and how much, is profitable. The fundamental fact which guides production, and in which the scarcity of capital expresses itself, is the price of input in terms of output, and this in turn depends on the proportion of income spent on consumers' goods compared with the proportion of income earned from the current production of consumers' goods. These proportions cannot be altered at will by adjustments in the money stream, since they depend on the one hand on the real quantities of the various types of goods in existence, and on the other hand on the way in which people will distribute their income between expenditure on consumers' goods and saving. Neither of these factors can be deliberately altered by monetary policy. As we have seen, any delay by monetary means of the adjustments made necessary by real changes can only have the effect of further accentuating these real changes, and any purely monetary change which in the first instance deflects interest rates in one direction is bound to set up forces which will ultimately change them in the opposite direction.

Significance of Rate of Saving

Ultimately, therefore, it is the rate of saving which sets the limits to the amount of investment that can be successfully carried through. But the effects of the rate of saving do not operate directly on the rate of interest or on the supply of investible funds, which will always be influenced largely by monetary factors. Its main influence is on the *demand* for investible funds, and here it operates in a direction opposite to that which is assumed by all the under-consumptionist theories. It will be *via* investment demand that a change in the rate of saving will affect the volume of investment. Similarly, it will be *via* investment demand that, if monetary influences should have caused investment to get out of step with saving, the balance will be restored. If throughout this discussion we have had little occasion to make explicit mention of the rate of saving, this is due to the fact that the effects considered will take place whatever the rate of saving, so long as this is a given magnitude and does not spontaneously change so as to restore the disrupted equilibrium. All that is required to make our analysis applicable is that, when incomes are increased by investment, the share of the additional income spent on consumers' goods during any period of time should be larger than the proportion by which the new investment adds to the output of consumers' goods during the same period of time. And there is of course no reason to expect that more than a fraction of the new income, and certainly not as much as has been newly invested, will be saved, because this would mean that practically all the income earned from the new investment would have to be saved.[6]

---

[6]The rate at which a given amount of new investment will contribute during any given interval of time to the output of consumers' goods stands of course in a very simple relation to the proportion between any new demand and the amount of investment to which it gives rise: the latter is simply the reciprocal value of the former. For a fuller discussion of the relationship between this 'quotient' and the 'multiplier' with which the 'acceleration principle of derived demand' operates I must again refer to Hayek (*Profits, Interest and Investment*, pp. 48–52).

It cannot be objected to this argument that, since investment automatically creates an identical amount of saving, the situation contemplated here cannot arise. The

The relative prices of the various types of goods and services, and therefore the rate of profit to be earned in their production, will always be determined by the impact of the monetary demand for the various kinds of goods and the supplies of these goods. And unless we study the factors limiting the supplies of these various types of goods,

---

irrelevant tautology, that *during any interval of time* the amount of income which has not been received from the sale of consumers' goods, and which therefore has been saved (namely, by those who spent that income), must have been spent on something other than consumers' goods (and therefore *ex definitione* must have been invested), is of little significance for this or for any other economic problem. What is relevant here is not the relation between one classification of money expenditure and another, but the relation of two streams of money expenditure to the streams of goods which they meet. We are interested in the amount of investment because it determines in what proportions (in terms of their relative costs) different kinds of goods will come into existence. And we are interested to know how these proportions between quantities of different kinds of goods are related to the proportions in which money expenditure will be distributed between the two kinds of goods, because it depends on the relation between these two proportions whether the production of either kind of good will become more or less profitable. It does not matter whether we put this question in the form of asking whether the distribution of income between expenditure on consumers' goods and saving corresponds to the proportion between the relative (replacement) *costs* of the total supply of consumers' goods and new investment goods, or whether the available resources are now distributed in the same proportion between the production of consumers' goods and the production of investment goods as those in which income earned from this production *will* be distributed between the two kinds of goods. Whichever of the two aspects of the question we prefer to stress, the essential thing, if we want to ask a meaningful question, is that we must always compare the result of investment embodied in concrete goods with the money expenditure on these goods. It is never the investment which is going on at the same time as the saving, but the result of *past* investment, that determines the supply of capital goods to which the monetary demand may or may not correspond. Playing about with the relationships between various classifications of total money expenditure during any given period will lead only to meaningless questions, and never to any result of the slightest relevance to any real problem.

I do not wish to suggest that the recent discussions of the various meanings of these concepts have been useless. They have helped us to make clear the conditions under which it is meaningful to talk about relations between saving and investment. But now that the obscurities and confusions connected with these concepts have been cleared up, the meaningless tautological use of these concepts ought clearly to disappear from scientific discussion. On the whole question, and the recent discussions about it, compare now the excellent exposition in the new Chapter 8 of the second edition of Professor Haberler's *Prosperity and Depression* (Geneva: League of Nations, 1939).

and particularly if we assume, as Mr. Keynes does, that they are all freely reproducible in practically unlimited quantities and without any appreciable lapse of time, we must remain in complete ignorance of the factors guiding production. In long-run equilibrium, the rate of profit and interest will depend on how much of their resources people want to use to satisfy their current needs, and how much they are willing to save and invest. But in the comparatively short run the quantities and kinds of consumers' goods and capital goods in existence must be regarded as fixed, and the rate of profit will depend not so much on the absolute quantity of real capital (however measured) in existence, or on the absolute height of the rate of saving, as on the relation between the proportion of the incomes spent on consumers' goods and the proportion of the resources available in the form of consumers' goods. For this reason it is quite possible that, after a period of great accumulation of capital and a high rate of saving, the rate of profit and the rate of interest may be higher than they were before—if the rate of saving is insufficient compared with the amount of capital which entrepreneurs have attempted to form, or if the demand for consumers' goods is too high compared with the supply. And for the same reason the rate of interest and profit may be higher in a rich community with much capital and a high rate of saving than in an otherwise similar community with little capital and a low rate of saving.

(*The Pure Theory of Capital,* pp. 393–96)

9. Dangers of the Short Run

This extract, the closing paragraphs of The Pure Theory of Capital, *concludes a long discussion of the interaction of real and monetary factors influencing interest-rate changes. Professor Hayek again stresses the superficiality of an analysis that confines itself to the immediate monetary impact of any policy and neglects its real long-term effects.*

The importance of the real factors is increasingly disregarded in contemporary discussion. But even without further continuing the discussion of the role money plays in this connection, we are certainly entitled to conclude from what we have already shown that the extent to which we can hope to shape events at will by controlling money is much more limited, that the scope of monetary policy is much more restricted, than is today widely believed. We cannot, as some writers seem to think, do more or less what we please with the economic system by playing on the monetary instrument. In every situation there will in fact always be only one monetary policy which will not have a disequilibrating effect and therefore eventually reverse its short-term influence. That it will always be exceedingly difficult, if not impossible, to know exactly what this policy is does not alter the fact that we cannot hope even to approach this ideal policy unless we understand not only the monetary but also, what are even more important, the real factors that are at work. There is little ground for believing that a system with the modern complex credit structure will ever work smoothly without some deliberate control of the monetary mechanism, since money by its very nature constitutes a kind of loose joint in the self-equilibrating apparatus of the price mechanism which is bound to impede its working—the more so the greater is the play in the loose joint. But the existence of such a loose joint is no justification for concentrating attention on that loose joint and disregarding the rest of the mechanism, and still less for making the greatest possible use of the short-lived freedom from economic necessity which the existence of this loose joint permits. On the contrary, the aim of any successful monetary policy must be to reduce as far as possible this slack in the self-correcting forces of the price mechanism, and to make adaptation more prompt so as to reduce the necessity for a later, more violent, reaction. For this, however, an understanding of the underlying real forces is even more important than an understanding of the monetary surface, just because this surface does not merely hide but often also disrupts the underlying mechanism in the most unexpected fashion. All this is not to deny that in the very short run the scope of monetary policy is very wide indeed. But the problem is not so much what we *can* do, but what we *ought* to do in the short run, and on this point a most harmful doctrine has gained ground in the last few years which can only be explained by a complete neglect—or complete lack of understanding—of the real forces at work. A policy has been advocated which at any moment aims at the maximum short-run effect of monetary policy, completely disregarding the fact that what is best in the short run may be extremely detrimental in the long run, because the indirect and slower effects of the short-run policy of the present shape the conditions, and limit the freedom, of the short-run policy of tomorrow and the day after.

Betrayal of Economists' Duty
I cannot help regarding the increasing concentration on short-run effects—which in this context amounts to the same thing as a concentration on purely monetary factors—not only as a serious and dangerous intellectual errors, but as a betrayal of the main duty of the economist and a grave menace to our civilisation. To the understanding of the forces which determine the day-to-day changes of business, the economist has probably little to contribute that the man of affairs does not know better. It used, however, to be regarded as the duty and the privilege of the economist to study and to stress the long-run effects which are apt to be hidden to the untrained eye, and to leave the concern about the more immediate effects to the practical man, who in any event would see only the latter and nothing else. The aim and effect of two hundred years of continuous development of economic thought have essentially been to lead us away from, and 'behind', the more superficial monetary mechanism and to bring out the real forces which guide long-run development. I do not wish to deny that the preoccupation with the 'real' as distinguished from the monetary aspects of the problems may sometimes have gone too far. But this can be no excuse for the present tendencies which have already gone far towards taking us back to the pre-scientific stage of

economics, when the whole working of the price mechanism was not yet understood, and only the problems of the impact of a varying money stream on a supply of goods and services with given prices aroused interest. It is not surprising that Mr. Keynes finds his views anticipated by the mercantilist writers and gifted amateurs: concern with the surface phenomena has always marked the first stage of the scientific approach to our subject. But it is alarming to see that after we have once gone through the process of developing a systematic account of those forces which in the long run determine prices and production, we are now called upon to scrap it, in order to replace it by the short-sighted philosophy of the business man raised to the dignity of a science. Are we not even told that, 'since in the long run we are all dead', policy should be guided entirely by short-run considerations? I fear that these believers in the principle of *après nous le déluge* may get what they have bargained for sooner than they wish.

(*The Pure Theory of Capital,* pp. 407–10)

IV. International versus National Policies

10. A Commodity Reserve Currency

In these two brief extracts Professor Hayek points to the advantages of an international economic system, and emphasises the necessity of an international monetary system for its proper functioning.

The gold standard as we knew it undoubtedly had some grave defects. But there is some danger that the sweeping condemnation of it which is now the fashion may obscure the fact that it also had some important virtues which most of the alternatives lack. A wisely and impartially controlled system of managed currency for the whole world might, indeed, be superior to it in all respects. But this is not a practical proposition for a long while yet. Compared, however, with the various schemes for monetary management on a national scale, the gold standard had three very important advantages: it created in effect an international currency without submitting national monetary policy to the decisions of an international authority; it made monetary policy in a great measure automatic and thereby predictable; and the changes in the supply of basic money which its mechanism secured were on the whole in the right direction.

    The importance of these advantages should not be lightly underestimated. The difficulties of a deliberate coordination of national policies are enormous, because our present knowledge gives us unambiguous guidance in only a few situations, and decisions in which nearly always some interests must be sacrificed to others will have to rest on subjective judgements. Uncoordinated national policies, however, directed solely by the immediate interests of the individual countries, may in their aggregate effect on every country well be worse than the most imperfect international standard. Similarly, though the automatic operation of the gold standard is far from perfect, the mere fact that under the gold standard policy is guided by known rules, and that, in consequence, the action of the authorities can be foreseen, may well make the imperfect gold standard less disturbing than a more rational but less comprehensible policy. The general principle that the production of gold is stimulated when its value begins to rise and discouraged when its value falls is right at least in the direction, if not in the way, in which it operates in practice.

An Irrational but Real Prestige
It will be noticed that none of these points claimed in favour of the gold standard is directly connected with any property inherent to gold. Any internationally accepted standard based on a commodity whose value is regulated by its cost of production would possess essentially the same advantages. What in the past made gold the only substance on which in practice an international standard could be based was mainly the irrational, but no less real factor of its prestige—or, if you will, of the ruling superstitious prejudice in favour of gold, which made it universally more acceptable than anything else. So long as this belief prevailed it was possible to maintain an international currency based on gold without much design or deliberate organisation to support it. But if it was prejudice which made the international gold standard possible, the existence of such a prejudice at least made an international money possible at a time when any international system based on explicit agreement and systematic cooperation was out of the question. It is probably true to say that all the rational arguments which can be advanced in favour of the gold standard apply even more strongly to this proposal, which is at the same time

free from most of the defects of the former. In judging the feasibility of the plan, it must, however, not be regarded solely as a scheme for currency reform. It must be borne in mind that the accumulation of commodity reserves is certain to remain part of national policy and that political considerations render it unlikely that the markets for raw commodities will in any future for which we can now plan be left entirely to themselves. All plans aiming at the direct control of the prices of particular commodities are, however, open to the most serious objections and certain to cause grave economic and political difficulties. Even apart from monetary consideration, the great need is for a system under which these controls are taken from the separate bodies which can but act in what is essentially an arbitrary and unpredictable manner and to make the controls instead subject to a mechanical and predictable rule. If this can be combined with the reconstruction of an international monetary system which would once more secure to the world stable international currency relations and a greater freedom in the movement of raw commodities, a great step would have been taken in the direction toward a more prosperous and stable world economy.

('A Commodity Reserve Currency', pp. 176–77, 184)

11. Keynes's Comment on Hayek

In a comment on Professor Hayek's article (No. 10) Keynes argues that an international monetary system is incompatible with 'nationally-determined' wage policies: i.e., the domestic restraint imposed by such an international system would be incompatible with the freedom of the organised trade union movement to determine wage-rates.

There are two complaints which it has been usual to lodge against a rigid gold standard as an instrument to secure stable prices. The first is that it does not provide the appropriate quantity of money. This is the familiar, old-fashioned criticism naturally put forward by adherents of the Quantity Theory. The way to meet it is, obviously, to devise a plan for varying appropriately the quantity of gold or its equivalent—for example, the tabular standard of Marshall sixty years ago, the compensated dollar of Irving Fisher forty years ago, or the commodity standard of Professor Hayek expounded in the article printed above.

The peculiar merit of the Clearing Union as a means of remedying a chronic shortage of international money is that it operates through the velocity, rather than through the volume, of circulation. A *volume* of money is only required to satisfy hoarding, to provide reserves against contingencies, and to cover inevitable time-lags between buying and spending. If hoarding is discouraged and if reserves against contingencies are provided by facultative overdrafts, a very small amount of actually outstanding credit might be sufficient for clearing between well-organised Central Banks. The CU, if it were fully successful, would deal with the quantity of international money by making any significant quantity unnecessary. The system might be improved, of course, by further increasing the discouragements to hoarding.

Conditions for National Price Stability

On another view, however, each national price-level is primarily determined by the relation of the national wage-level to the national efficiency; or, more generally, by the relation of money-costs to efficiency in terms of the national unit of currency. And if price-levels are determined by money-costs, it follows that whilst an appropriate quantity of money is a *necessary* condition of stable prices, it is not a *sufficient* condition. For prices can only be stabilised by first stabilising the relation of money-wages (and other costs) to efficiency.

The second (and more modern) complaint against the gold standard is, therefore, that it attempts to confine the natural tendency of wages to rise beyond the limits set by the volume of money, but can only do so by the weapon of deliberately creating unemployment. This weapon the world, after a good try, has decided to discard. And this complaint may be just as valid against a new standard which aims at providing the quantity of money appropriate to stable prices, as it is against the old gold standard.

In the field of price stabilisation international currency projects have, therefore, as I conceive it, only a limited objective. They do not aim at stable prices as such. For international prices which are stable in terms of unitas or bancor cannot be translated into stable national price-levels except by the old gold standard methods of influencing the level of domestic money-costs. And, failing this, there is not much point in an international price-level providing stability in terms of an international unit which is not reflected in a corresponding stability of the actual price-levels of member countries.

Different National Policies Needed

The primary aim of an international currency scheme should be, therefore, to prevent not only those evils which result from a chronic shortage of international money due to the draining of gold into creditor countries but also those which follow from countries failing to maintain stability of domestic efficiency-costs and moving out of step with one another in their national wage-policies without having at their disposal any means of orderly adjustment. And if orderly adjustment is allowed, that is another way of saying that countries may be allowed by the scheme, which is not the case with the gold standard, to pursue, if they choose, different wage policies and, therefore, different price policies.

Thus the more difficult task of an international currency scheme, which will only be fully solved with the aid of experience, is to deal with the problem of members getting out of step in their domestic wage and credit policies. To meet this it can be provided that countries seriously out of step (whether too fast or too slow) may be asked in the first instance to reconsider their policies. But, if necessary (and it will be necessary, if efficiency wage-rates move at materially different rates), exchange rates will have to be altered so as to reconcile a particular national policy to the average pace. If the initial exchange-rates are fixed correctly, this is likely to be the only important disequilibrium for which a change in exchange rates is the appropriate remedy.

It follows that an international currency scheme can work to perfection within the field of maintaining exchange stability, and yet prices may move substantially. If wages and prices double everywhere alike, international exchange equilibrium is undisturbed. If efficiency wage-rates in a particular country rise ten percent more than the norm, then it is that there is trouble which needs attention.

The fundamental reason for thus limiting the objectives of an international currency scheme is the impossibility, or at any rate, the undesirability, of imposing stable price-levels from without. The error of the gold standard lay in submitting national wage-policies to outside dictation. It is wiser to regard stability (or otherwise) of internal prices as a matter of internal policy and politics. Commodity standards which try to impose this from without will break down just as surely as the rigid gold-standard.

Some countries are likely to be more successful than others in preserving stability of internal prices and efficiency wages—and it is the offsetting of that inequality of success which will provide an international organisation with its worst headaches. A communist country is in a position to be very successful. Some people argue that a capitalist country is doomed to failure because it will be found impossible in conditions of full employment to prevent a progressive increase of wages. According to this view severe slumps and recurrent periods of unemployment have been hitherto the only effective means of holding efficiency wages within a reasonably stable range. Whether this is so remains to be seen. The more conscious we are of this problem, the likelier shall we be to surmount it.

('The Objective of International Price Stability', pp. 185–87)

12. F.D. Graham's Criticism of Keynes

Professor F.D. Graham, in a comment on Keynes's criticism, indicated the full inflationary implications of Keynes's ideas; in the economic system Keynes envisaged, monetary policy would be subordinated to the wage-rate policies followed by the unions, so that the politically powerful were enabled to exploit the politically weak (since those who were unable to raise their incomes along with the trade unionists would have to face ever-increasing prices on static or more slowly rising incomes). Professor Graham's essay is notable for its early exposition of this important consideration.

The issues raised in Lord Keynes's reply to Professor F.A. Hayek's article on a commodity reserve currency, in a recent issue of *Economic Journal*, seem worthy of more extended discussion.[1]

It will perhaps do no great injustice to Professor Hayek's views to assert that he brought the great weight of his authority to an all but unqualified support of the proposal to give free coinage to warehouse receipts covering representative bales of the standard storable raw materials of industry and trade.[2]

Professor Hayek believes that the defects of the gold standard lay not in conception, but in adequacy to its task. The gold standard always operated in the right direction, but not with sufficient power or speed. Whenever the public showed an increasing preference for liquidity—with a consequent fall in the price level—the mining of gold was stimulated in compensation of the unemployment with which other industries were then afflicted. But the relative unimportance of gold mining as an employer of labour, or its complete absence from many economies, reduced this compensation to negligible importance

---

[1] Professor Hayek's article, 'A Commodity Reserve Currency', was followed by Lord Keynes's reply, 'The Objective of International Price Stability', *Economic Journal* LIII, Nos. 210–11 (June–September, 1943): 176–87.

[2] The proposal is elaborated by its initiator, Mr. Benjamin Graham, in his book *Storage and Stability* (New York: McGraw-Hill, 1937), and is now so well known as not to require further exposition here.

everywhere but in South Africa. The gold standard also operated, at long last, to check any secular trend in the price level through the increase in the rate of gold supply which attended a rise in the real value of gold, and the reduction in the rate of gold supply which occurred when the real value of gold fell off. But, if the nineteenth century may be taken as a criterion, the attendant 'cycle' takes something like a quarter of a century to run its course.

Though the gold standard thus tended towards the maintenance of full employment, and to the preservation of a stable price level, the tendency in both cases was so faint as to be of no practical importance. Professor Hayek and other advocates of a commodity reserve standard assert that it would greatly ameliorate, if not completely cure, these defects of adequacy in its gold counterpart.

The 'Natural Tendency of Wages'

Lord Keynes, I take it, is not concerned to deny these asserted virtues of a commodity reserve standard, but says that it is open, along with the gold standard, to another, more modern and, one gathers, more important, objection, in that it would attempt 'to confine the natural tendency of wages to rise beyond the limits set by the volume of money', and that it could do so only by deliberately creating unemployment.

I do not know what Lord Keynes means by the 'natural' tendency of wages to rise beyond the limits set by the volume of money, unless it is that the wage-earner would always like to have higher money wages than he can currently earn on the basis of a stable price level, and that no one is in a position to prevent his getting them. This would certainly be news to Karl Marx, and if both Marx and Keynes were right in their day and generation, the proletariat has surely come into its own, and more, in a way that Marx never envisaged. The degree in which it is true that there is any 'natural' tendency towards an increase of money wages per unit of output is, of course, a matter of time, place and circumstance, and what should be done about it, in any given case, is a political rather than an economic problem. The problem, that is, does not at all touch the question as to whether the commodity reserve standard is an economically good monetary standard, but is solely concerned with its reception by a politically potent group.

That Lord Keynes is under no illusions about the dangers of appeasement of such a group is shown by the fact that, in his concluding paragraph, he says that 'some people argue that a capitalist country is doomed to failure because it will be found impossible in conditions of full employment to prevent a progressive increase in wages' (beyond the point which can be sustained without a persistent rise in the price level). Disregarding the query as to whether a country so situated could be called 'capitalist', rather than under the domination of a not very enlightened proletariat, it may, perhaps, be at once conceded that there is much to be said for Lord Keynes's contention that, in dealing with the problem, it is essential that any given country have sovereignty over its own monetary arrangements. His opposition to an international stabilisation of prices, imposed from outside on all participating countries, applies, of course, to an international commodity reserve standard with fixed exchange rates. (It applies still more strongly to an international system of *unstable* prices, with fixed or viscous exchange-rate relationships, since the international price level might then fall rather than rise and would, in any case, inevitably fail to correspond with the varying shifts in independently determined efficiency-wage rates in the several countries.) Since Lord Keynes justifiably believes that the difficulty of securing the allegiance of the wage-earning group to a policy of stable national price levels would be greatly enhanced if it could be made to appear that such a policy was the result of an international convention, rather than of purely national interest, he looks askance at what he believes to be a proposal, through international action, to fasten stable price levels on all participating countries.

Gold Standard 'Dictation'

Lord Keynes, however, is, I think, not right in saying that 'the error of the gold standard lay in submitting national wage-policies to outside dictation'. The original gold standard did not submit wage-policies to *dictation,* by governing authority anywhere, but made them the resultant of impersonal forces issuing out of the disposition, and potentiality, of individuals to follow what they conceived to be their own interest. This system, as Professor Hayek points out, had many virtues, and we should be badly advised if we should throw away its virtues along with its imperfections. The automaticity of the gold standard was, *per se,* all to the good, and what we need is a similarly automatic system which will be free of the vices of the traditional gold standard. We should not forget that the once well-nigh universal adhesion to the gold standard was spontaneous rather than imposed, and that it was only *after* the gold standard had been subjected to varying national management, in an attempt to overcome the original objections against it, that it was abandoned by those countries that could not make their ideas on its management effective, that is, after (unstable) price levels had been imposed from without.

Lord Keynes's assertion that a commodity reserve standard imposed from without (such as he supposes Professor Hayek to endorse) would break down just as surely as the rigid gold standard, is not obviously true, but I am not concerned to dispute it.[3] Professor Hayek, in his article, fails to state explicitly whether or not he posits fixed exchange rates of all national currencies against the international commodity standard and, therefore, against each other. But if, in line with Professor Hayek's suggestion, some international organisation, such as, *e.g.,* the new 'Fund' or the Bank for International Settlements, should offer freely to exchange, both ways, an international currency unit against warehouse receipts covering a designated composite of raw materials,

---

[3] The reason that it is not obviously true is that a policy of stable price levels would, I believe, prove to be much more generally acceptable than the caprices of the unmanaged gold standard or the arbitrariness of that standard in its managed form.

no monetary policy would thereby be *imposed* on any country. So far as any country chose to keep the exchange value of its own currency fixed, against the international unit and other currencies tied to it, it would automatically have a substantially stable price level. So far, however, as, for one reason or another, it preferred an unstabilised price level, the exchange value of its currency, *vis-à-vis* the international unit and the currencies of countries with stable exchange rates against that unit, would, as a result of commodity arbitrage, automatically shift in strictly appropriate correspondence with its shifting domestic purchasing power. It seems to me, therefore, that Lord Keynes's argument that an international commodity reserve currency would *impose,* from without, a price-level policy on any country, or would break down, is quite untenable.

There would seem to be no reason why an international monetary unit of this sort should not be the international currency around which the operations of a Clearing Union, on Lord Keynes's lines, or any international fund, could be centred. Through the concurrent free purchase and sale of gold, at a fixed price in the international currency, the gold value of the international unit could also be fixed, or, what is the same thing, the commodity value of gold would be stabilised. This would avoid all the controversy which would be involved in any proposal to deprive gold of its present, or traditional, functions.

Such a standard would represent a great advance over anything we have had in the past. Not only would it be of great value in connection with international investment, but it would furnish a *point d'appui* to which any country desirous of stable price levels, and of fixed exchange rates with other like-minded countries, could, by linking its own currency to the international unit through purchase and sale at fixed prices, repair.

Unanchored Medium of Exchange

When once a tie with any and every asset, or group of assets, is abandoned, and resort is had to a pure debt currency, one has, in my judgement, no *standard* at all, but merely a wholly unanchored medium of exchange and unit of account. Though I have the fullest sympathy with the wage-earner's getting the highest (real) wages possible, in the current state of the industrial arts, it seems to me that any monetary policy which does not confine such tendency as (money) wages may have to rise beyond the limits within which it is possible to preserve a stable price level, provides a very vicious 'standard'. If Lord Keynes takes the contrary view, he seems to me, in effect, to be plumping for a progressive inflation, wholly indefinite as to time and amount. Against any argument for such a currency I would assert that movements in the price *level* have no functional significance, or that, if they have, we cannot hope to run a satisfactory economic system with price as the regulating mechanism. In that case, the more quickly we go to some not very limited form of responsible totalitarianism the better it will be for all concerned. If we cannot have a distributorily neutral money, any group that can get control of the monetary system will have totalitarian power over the lives and fortunes of their fellows, without any clear recognition of responsibility.

In a perfectly free monetary system, there is, of course, no rate of money wages which would ever, of itself, bring unemployment, since there is nothing to prevent commodity prices from rising (under the stimulus of new issues of money) to whatever level is necessary to cover the stepped-up money cost of the labour factor of production. All of us, moreover, are impatient with the senseless unemployment with which we have so long been afflicted. But, if we refuse even to accept the threat of unemployment under any conditions whatever, we shall, under any 'natural' tendency of money wages to rise faster than efficiency, be forced to pay whatever money wages labourers may be pleased to demand and to jack up the price level unendingly to take care of the situation. The knowledge of what unlimited inflation can mean would seem to preclude the prevention, in this way, of a mote of unemployment.

A commodity reserve currency would operate to provide unlimited employment, through the unlimited demand for the commodities in the reserve, provided the workers did not seek to drive money wages above the figure which, at a stable price level, is warranted by their real productivity. They are entitled to so much—not less and not more—and, if we shrink from saying 'No' when they press their demands beyond this point, we shall no longer have an economic system, but merely a racket. One may contend, if he will, that to say 'No' is a deliberate induction of unemployment, but the answer is that employment will be available if the workers refrain from pushing what, in the circumstances, are quite impossible demands for higher (real) wages. Higher money wages, if granted in the circumstances, would do the workers no good as consumers, since such wages must be compensated by a higher price level, and, even if some slight unemployment were thus prevented, it would be at devastating cost in social freedom.

The Real Problem of Unemployment
Our real problem of unemployment is not that people are denied the opportunity of work at whatever fancy wage they may desire, but that they are denied that opportunity at wages that they could readily earn under conditions of normal liquidity preference. It is the merit of commodity reserves that they would operate to keep the preference for liquidity from rising, or would sate the appetite for it, by offering it freely in such a way as not to interfere with production.

It is true, as Lord Keynes says, that 'prices can only be stabilised by first stabilising the relation of money wages (and other costs) to efficiency'. This is precisely the purpose of commodity reserve money, and I can see no reason for not pursuing it. As the efficiency of labour rises, money wages would tend to rise in correspondence—no more and no less—and there would be a steady tendency towards full employment without a trace of inflation.

It is also true that 'international prices which are stable in terms of unitas or bancor [the international unit] cannot be translated into stable national price-levels except by . . . influencing the level of domestic money-costs'. Domestic money-costs would be so influenced, under fixed rates of exchange of a national currency against the international commodity unit, and I see no strong reason for objecting to this consequence. Whatever the objections, or lack of them, the influence would, in any case, not be present if, as pointed out above, the exchange rate of the national against the international unit were left free to move in correspondence with variations in the local currency price of the commodity composite relative to the fixed price in the international currency.[4] If one insists upon an unstabilised price level at home, there is nothing in a stabilised international unit to prevent it, or nothing to prevent other countries having stable price levels if they so desire. No country, therefore, would be any more inhibited in the presence of an international monetary unit of stable value than in the presence of an international unit without anchor, and a stable-value international unit would not interfere in any way with anything that Lord Keynes has proposed in his Clearing Union.

Professor Hayek's 'Intransigence'
It is the intransigence of the attitude taken here, and by Professor Hayek, which is, I think, troubling Lord Keynes. To him it seems ruthless to accept, or provoke, unemployment as a means of enforcing adherence to pecuniary purity. How much otherwise avoidable unemployment, he asks, would you be willing to bring about for this purpose?[5] The query reflects not only Lord Keynes's humanitarian concern, but also his doubts as to political possibilities. He thinks

---

[4]This whole matter is treated in detail in my brochure *Fundamentals of International Monetary Policy,* International Finance Section, Department of Economics and Social Institutions, Princeton University, No. 2.

[5]The question was raised in private correspondence with the author.

that other, less punitive, means must be found if the desired end is to be attained. It would be churlish, and foolish, to deny the cogency of his objections on this point, and the answer, I think, lies in the adoption of a minimum wage policy with a normal yearly increase in the minimum equal to a generously computed expectation of enhancement in the general level of efficiency. Experience goes to show that wages above the minimum will respond, at least proportionately, to any increase in the lowest group, and if, at any time, the expectation of improvement in general efficiency were shown to be over-computed (by the fact or immediate threat of unemployment in the industries producing the goods in the commodity unit), the stated increase in the minimum wage should be temporarily suspended in accordance with appropriate provisions in the legislation. Some such measures as this would reduce the acerbity of disputes over the distribution of income and would promote adjustments in an orderly rather than chaotic manner.

So long as our economic system deviates widely, and in certain respects progressively, from ideally free competition, there is bound to be some friction in the determination of who gets what, and why. So long, moreover, as we preserve anything whatever of the spirit of free contract, the enterpriser must be as free to reject the demands of workers as are the latter to reject the terms that the enterpriser may offer. Any unemployment that may result from this cause is an inevitable phase of freedom. It would be as fatal to freedom to insist that, to avoid any unemployment whatever, the enterpriser must pay whatever monetary wages organised workers may demand, and that the State must so shape its monetary policy as to make this possible, as it would be to insist, to the same end, that workers must accept whatever monetary wage a fascist group of employers might see fit to impose.

('Keynes vs. Hayek on a Commodity Reserve Currency', pp. 422–28)

13. KEYNES'S REPLY TO GRAHAM

In his reply to F.D. Graham, Keynes failed to take up the major issue that had been raised: that of allowing monetary policy to be used as a supplement to union wage-rate fixing. Indeed, Keynes continued to assume that prices, as a normal course, would be adjusted to whatever wage-rates unions succeeded in obtaining, i.e., he assumed a continuous inflation.

Professor Graham's statement of my point of view is a very fair one. But in the note on which he comments I expressed myself much more briefly than the nature of the subject matter really allowed. So, to diminish the chances of misunderstandings, there are one or two points I should like to restate and emphasise.

I have no quarrel with a tabular standard as being intrinsically more sensible than gold. My own sympathies have always fallen that way. I hope the world will come to some version of it some time. But the opinion I was expressing was on the level of contemporary practical policy; and on that level I do not feel that this is the next urgent thing or that other measures should be risked or postponed for the sake of it. These are some of my reasons:

1. The immediate task is to discover some orderly, yet elastic, method of linking national currencies to an international currency, whatever the type of international currency may be. So long as national currencies change their values out of step with one another, I doubt if this task is made easier by substituting a tabular standard for gold. Indeed the task of getting an *elastic* procedure may be made more difficult, since a tabular standard might make rigidity seem more plausible. Perhaps unjustly, I was suspecting Professor Hayek of seeking a new way to satisfy a propensity towards a rigid system.

2. In particular, I doubt the political wisdom of appearing, more than is inevitable in any orderly system, to impose an external pressure on national standards and therefore on wage levels. Of course, I do not want to see money wages forever soaring upwards to a level to

which real wages cannot follow. It is one of the chief tasks ahead of our statesmanship to find a way to prevent this. But we must solve it in our own domestic way, feeling that we are free men, free to be wise or foolish. The suggestion of *external* pressure will make the difficult psychological and political problem of making good sense prevail still more difficult.

3. This does not strike me as an opportune moment to attack the vested interests of gold holders and gold producers. Why waste one's breath on what the Governments of the United States, Russia, Western Europe and the British Commonwealth are bound to reject?

4. The right way to approach the tabular standard is to evolve a technique and to accustom men's minds to the idea through international buffer stocks. When we have thoroughly mastered the technique of these, which is sufficiently difficult without the further complications of the tabular standard and the oppositions and prejudices which this must overcome, it will be time enough to think again. On buffer stocks I can enthusiastically join forces with Professor Frank Graham and Mr. Benjamin Graham. Though even here I am beginning to feel a slight reserve about whether just this moment, when many materials are scarce, is the right moment to start; they can so easily be turned into producers' ramps, and if they start that way the prospect of a brilliant improvement will have been prejudiced.

All this, I agree, is very low-level talk; for which I apologise. But it was in fact from a low level that I was, in the first instance, addressing Professor Hayek on his dolomite.

('Note by Lord Keynes', pp. 429–30)

V. Wage Rigidities and Inflation

14. Full Employment, Planning and Inflation

Professor Hayek here develops one of his main themes. Save in the exceptional circumstances of the general unemployment of all factors of production, the 'unemployment' problem is one of securing the right distribution of labour; monetary expansion along Keynesian lines, by nullifying the effects of relative price movements, exacerbates the situation and makes it impossible to maintain any given volume of employment, except by continued inflation. Considerations such as these are not clearly grasped within the 'bloc' thinking of the macro-approach, which may thus serve to conceal important aspects of reality.

In the years that have elapsed since the war, central planning, 'full employment', and inflationary pressure have been the three features which have dominated economic policy in the greater part of the world. Of these only full employment can be regarded as desirable in itself. Central planning, direction, or government controls, however we care to call it, is at best a means which must be judged by the results. Inflation, even 'repressed inflation', is undoubtedly an evil, though some would say a necessary evil if other desirable aims are to be achieved. It is part of the price we pay for having committed ourselves to a policy of full employment and central planning.

The new fact which has brought about this situation is not a greater desire to avoid unemployment than existed before the war. It is the new belief that a higher level of employment can be permanently maintained by monetary pressure than would be possible without it. The pursuit of a policy based on these beliefs has somewhat unexpectedly shown that inflation and government controls are its necessary accompaniments—unexpected not by all, but by probably the majority of those who advocated those policies.

Full Employment the Main Priority
Full employment policies as now understood are thus the dominant factor of which the other characteristic features of contemporary economic policy are mainly the consequence. Before we can further examine the manner in which central planning, full employment, and inflation interact, we must become clear about what precisely the full employment policies as now practised mean.

Full employment has come to mean that maximum of employment that can be brought about in the short run by monetary pressure. This may not be the original meaning of the theoretical concept, but it was inevitable that it should have come to mean this in practice. Once it was admitted that the momentary state of employment should form the main guide to monetary policy, it was inevitable that any degree of unemployment which might be removed by monetary pressure should be regarded as sufficient justification for applying such pressure. That in most situations employment can be temporarily increased by monetary expansion has long been known. If this possibility has not always been used, this was because it was thought that by such measures not only other dangers were created, but that long-term stability of employment itself might be endangered by them. What is new about present beliefs is that it is now widely held that so long as monetary expansion creates additional employment, it is innocuous or at least will cause more benefit than harm.

Yet while in practice full employment policies merely mean that in the short run employment is kept somewhat higher than it would otherwise be, it is at least doubtful whether over longer periods they will not in fact lower the level of employment which can be permanently maintained without progressive monetary expansion. These policies are, however, constantly represented as if the practical problem were not this, but as if the choice were between full employment thus defined and the lasting mass unemployment of the 1930s.

The habit of thinking in terms of an alternative between 'full employment' and a state of affairs in which there are unemployed factors of all kinds available is perhaps the most dangerous legacy which we owe to the great influence of the late Lord Keynes. That so long as a state of general unemployment prevails, in the sense that unused resources of *all* kinds exist, monetary expansion can be only beneficial, few people will deny. But such a state of general unemployment is something rather exceptional, and it is by no means evident that a policy which will be beneficial in such a state will also always and necessarily be so in the kind of intermediate position in which an economic system finds itself most of the time, when significant unemployment is confined to certain industries, occupations or localities.

Unemployment and Inadequate Demand
Of a system in a state of general unemployment it is roughly true that employment will fluctuate in proportion with money income, and that if we succeed in increasing money income we shall also in the same proportion increase employment. But it is just not true that all unemployment is in this manner due to an insufficiency of aggregate demand and can be lastingly cured by increasing demand. The causal connection between income and employment is not a simple one-way connection so that by raising income by a certain ratio we can always raise employment by the same ratio. It is all too naïve a way of thinking to believe that, since, if all workmen were employed at current wages, total income would reach such and such a figure, therefore, if we can bring income to that figure, we shall also necessarily have full employment. Where unemployment is not evenly

spread, there is no certainty that additional expenditure will go where it will create additional employment. At least the amount of extra expenditure which would have to be incurred before the demand for the kind of services is raised which the unemployed offer may have to be of such a magnitude as to produce major inflationary effects before it substantially increases employment.

If expenditure is distributed between industries and occupations in a proportion different from that in which labour is distributed, a mere increase in expenditure need not increase employment. Unemployment can evidently be the consequence of the fact that the distribution of labour is different from the distribution of demand. In this case the low aggregate money income would have to be considered as a consequence rather than as a cause of unemployment. Even though, during the process of increasing incomes, enough expenditure may 'spill over' into the depressed sectors temporarily there to cure unemployment, as soon as the expansion comes to an end the discrepancy between the distribution of demand and the distribution of supply will again show itself. Where the cause of unemployment and of low aggregate incomes is such a discrepancy, only a reallocation of labour can lastingly solve the problem in a free economy.

This raises one of the most crucial and most difficult problems in the whole field: is an inappropriate distribution of labour more likely to be corrected under more or less stable or under expanding monetary conditions? This involves in fact two separate problems: the first is whether demand conditions during a process of expansion are such that, if the distribution of labour adjusted itself to the then existing distribution of demand, this would create employment which would continue after expansion has stopped; the second problem is whether the distribution of labour is more likely to adapt itself promptly to any given distribution of demand under stable or under expansionary monetary conditions, or, in other words, whether labour is more mobile under expanding or under stable monetary conditions.

The answer to the first of these questions is fairly clear. During a process of expansion the direction of demand is to some extent necessarily different from what it will be after expansion has stopped. Labour will be attracted to the particular occupations on which the extra expenditure is made in the first instance. So long as expansion lasts, demand there will always run a step ahead of the consequential increases of demand elsewhere. And in so far as this temporary stimulus to demand in particular sectors leads to a movement of labour, it may well become the cause of unemployment as soon as the expansion comes to an end.

Main Cause of Recurrent Unemployment

Some people may feel doubt about the importance of this phenomenon. To the present writer it seems the main cause of the recurrent waves of unemployment. That during every boom period a greater quantity of factors of production is drawn into the capital goods industries than can be permanently employed there, and that as a result we have normally a greater proportion of our resources specialised in the production of capital goods than corresponds to the share of income which, under full employment, will be saved and be available for investment, seems to him the cause of the collapse which has regularly followed a boom. Any attempt to create full employment by drawing labour into occupations where they will remain employed only so long as credit expansion continues creates the dilemma that either credit expansion must be continued indefinitely (which means inflation), or that, when it stops, unemployment will be greater than it would be if the temporary increase in employment had never taken place.

If the real cause of unemployment is that the distribution of labour does not correspond with the distribution of demand, the only way to create stable conditions of high employment which is not dependent on continued inflation (or physical controls) is to bring about a distribution of labour which matches the manner in which a stable money income will be spent. This depends of course not only on whether during the process of adaptation the distribution of demand is approximately what it will remain, but also on whether conditions in general are conducive to easy and rapid movements of labour.

This leads to the second and more difficult part of our question to which, perhaps, no certain answer can be given, though the probability seems to us to point clearly in one direction. This is the question whether workers will on the whole be more willing to move to new occupations or new localities when general demand is rising, or whether mobility is likely to be greater when total demand is approximately constant. The main difference between the two cases is that in the former the inducement to move will be the attraction of a higher wage elsewhere, while in the second case it will be the inability to earn the accustomed wages or to find any employment in the former occupation which will exercise a push. The former method is, of course, the more pleasant, and it is usually also represented as the more effective. It is this latter belief which I am inclined to question.

That the same wage differentials which in the long run would attract the necessary greater number of new recruits to one industry rather than another will not suffice to tempt workers already established in the latter to move is in itself not surprising. As a rule the movement from job to job involves expenditure and sacrifices which may not be justified by a mere increase in wages. So long as the worker can count on his accustomed money wage in his current job, he will be understandably reluctant to move. Even if, as would be inevitable under an expansionist policy which aimed at bringing about the adjustment entirely by raising some wages without allowing others to fall, the constant money wages meant a lower real wage, the habit of thinking in terms of money wages would deprive such a fall of real wages of most of its effectiveness. It is curious that those disciples of Lord Keynes who in other connections make such constant use of this consideration regularly fail to see its significance in this context.

To aim at securing to men who in the social interest ought to move elsewhere the continued receipt of their former wages can only delay movements which ultimately must take place. It should also not be forgotten that in order to give all the men formerly employed continued employment in a relatively declining industry, the general level of wages in that industry will have to fall more than would be necessary if some of the workers moved away from it.

What is so difficult here for the layman to understand is that to protect the individual against the loss of his job may not be a way to decrease unemployment but may over longer periods rather decrease the number which can be employed at given wages. If a policy is pursued over a long period which postpones and delays movements, which keeps people in their old jobs who ought to move elsewhere, the result must be that what ought to have been a gradual process of change becomes in the end a problem of the necessity of mass transfers within a short period. Continued monetary pressure which has helped people to earn an unchanged money wage in jobs which they ought to have left will have created accumulated arrears of necessary changes which, as soon as monetary pressure ceases, will have to be made up in a much shorter space of time and then result in a period of acute mass unemployment which might have been avoided.

Expansion May Hinder Adjustment
All this applies not only to those maldistributions of labour which arise in the course of ordinary industrial fluctuations, but even more to the task of large-scale reallocations of labour such as arise after a great war or as a result of a major change in the channels of international trade. It seems highly doubtful whether the expansionist policies pursued since the war in most countries have helped and not rather hindered that adjustment to radically changed conditions of world trade which have become necessary. Especially in the case of Great Britain the low unemployment figures during recent years may be more a sign of a delay in necessary change than of true economic balance.

The great problem in all those instances is whether such a policy, once it has been pursued for years, can still be reversed without serious political and social disturbances. As a result of these policies, what not very long ago might merely have meant a slightly higher unemployment figure, might now, when the employment of large numbers has become dependent on the continuation of these policies, be indeed an experiment which politically is unbearable.

Full employment policies, as at present practised, attempt the quick and easy way of giving men employment where they happen to be, while the real problem is to bring about a distribution of labour which makes continuous high employment without artificial stimulus possible. What this distribution is we can never know beforehand. The only way to find out is to let the unhampered market act under conditions which will bring about a stable equilibrium between demand and supply. But the very full employment policies make it almost inevitable that we must constantly interfere with the free play of the forces of the market and that the prices which rule during such an expansionary policy, and to which supply will adapt itself, will not represent a lasting condition. These difficulties, as we have seen, arise from the fact that unemployment is never evenly spread throughout the economic system, but that, at the time when there may still be substantial unemployment in some sectors, there may exist acute scarcities in others. The purely fiscal and monetary measures on which current full employment policies rely are, however, by themselves indiscriminate in their effects on the different parts of the economic system. The same monetary pressure which in some parts of the system might merely reduce unemployment will in others produce definite inflationary effects. If not checked by other measures, such monetary pressure might well set up an inflationary spiral of prices and wages long before unemployment has disappeared, and—with present nationwide wage bargaining—the rise of wages may threaten the results of the full employment policy even before it has been achieved.

As is regularly the case in such circumstances, the governments will then find themselves forced to take measures to counteract the effects of their own policy. The effects of the inflation have to be contained or 'repressed' by direct controls of prices and of quantities produced and sold: the rise of prices has to be prevented by imposing maximum prices and the resulting scarcities must be met by a system of rationing, priorities and allocations.

The manner in which inflation leads a government into a system of overall controls and central planning is by now too well known to need elaboration. It is usually a particularly pernicious kind of planning, because not thought out beforehand but applied piecemeal as the unwelcome results of inflation manifest themselves. A government which uses inflation as an instrument of policy but wants it to produce only the desired effects is soon driven to control ever increasing parts of the economy.

(*Studies in Philosophy, Politics and Economics,* pp. 270–76)

15. INFLATION RESULTING FROM DOWNWARD INFLEXIBILITY OF WAGES

Professor Hayek reiterates the central role of wage rates in determining the volume of employment. Reasoning in terms of wage levels *rather than in terms of the structure of wage rates obscures the inflationary implications of refusing to reduce wage rates where necessary. If union-determined wage rates are treated as the datum to which all other economic values must adjust themselves, the monetary consequences of such a course must be clearly recognised. If we wish to avoid the latter, trade unions must treat the flow of money incomes as the final datum to which they must adjust their wage rates. Professor Hayek here explicitly and unambiguously analyses the specific interactions of union wage policy and official monetary policy in creating one of the major dilemmas facing the developed economies.*

Contrary to what is widely believed, the crucial result of the 'Keynesian Revolution' is the general acceptance of a factual assumption and, what is more, of an assumption which becomes true as a result of its being generally accepted. The Keynesian theory, as it has developed during the last twenty years, has become a formal apparatus which may or may not be more convenient to deal with the facts than classical monetary theory; this is not our concern here. The decisive assumption on which Keynes's original argument rested and which has since ruled policy is that it is impossible ever to reduce the money wages of a substantial group of workers without causing extensive unemployment. The conclusion which Lord Keynes drew from this, and which the whole of his theoretical system was intended to justify, was that since money wages can in practice not be lowered, the adjustment necessary, whenever wages have become too high to allow 'full employment', must be effected by the devious process of reducing the value of money. A society which accepts this is bound for a continuous process of inflation.

Importance of Relative Wages
This consequence is not at once apparent within the Keynesian system because Keynes and most of his followers are arguing in terms of a general wage level while the chief problem appears only if we think in terms of the relative wages of the different (sectional or regional) groups of workers. Relative wages of the different groups are bound to change substantially in the course of economic development. But if the money wage of no important group is to fall, the adjustment of the relative position must be brought about exclusively by raising all other money wages. The effect must be a continuous rise in the level of money wages greater than the rise of real wages, i.e., inflation. One need only consider the normal year-by-year dispersion of wage changes of the different groups in order to realise how important this factor must be.

The twelve years since the end of the war have in fact in the whole Western world been a period of more or less continuous inflation. It does not matter how far this was entirely the result of deliberate policy or the product of the exigencies of government finance. It certainly has been a very popular policy since it has been accompanied by great prosperity over a period of probably unprecedented length. The great problem is whether by the same means prosperity can be maintained indefinitely—or whether an attempt to do so is not bound sooner or later to produce other results which in the end must become unbearable.

The point which tends to be overlooked in current discussion is that inflation acts as a stimulus to business only in so far as it is unforeseen, or greater than expected. Rising prices by themselves, as has often been seen, are not necessarily a guarantee of prosperity. Prices must turn out to be higher than they were expected to be, in order to produce profits larger than normal. Once a further rise of prices is expected with certainty, competition for the factors of production will drive up costs in anticipation. If prices rise no more than expected there will be no extra profits, and if they rise less, the effect will be the same as if prices fell when they had been expected to be stable.

On the whole the post-war inflation has been unexpected or has lasted longer than expected. But the longer inflation lasts, the more it will be generally expected to continue; and the more people count on a continued rise of prices, the more must prices rise in order to secure adequate profits not only to those who would earn them without inflation but also to those who would not. Inflation greater than expected secures general prosperity only because those who without it would make no profit and be forced to turn to something else are enabled to continue with their present activities. A cumulative inflation at a progressive rate will probably secure prosperity for a fairly long time, but not inflation at a constant rate. We need hardly inquire why inflation at a progressive rate cannot be continued indefinitely: long before it becomes so fast as to make any reasonable calculation in the expanding currency impracticable and before it will be spontaneously replaced by some other medium of exchange, the inconvenience and injustice of the rapidly falling value of all fixed payments will produce irresistible demands for a halt—irresistible, at least, when people understand what is happening and realise that a government can always stop inflation. (The hyper-inflations after the First World War were tolerated only because people were deluded into believing that the increase of the quantity of money was not a cause but a necessary consequence of the rise of prices.)

We can therefore not expect inflation-borne prosperity to last indefinitely. We are bound to reach a point at which the source of prosperity which inflation now constitutes will no longer be available. Nobody can predict when this point will be reached, but come it will. Few things should give us greater concern than the need to secure an arrangement of our productive resources which we can hope to maintain at a reasonable level of activity and employment when the stimulus of inflation ceases to operate.

Inflation—A Vicious Circle
Yet the longer we have relied on inflationary expansion to secure prosperity, the more difficult that task will be. We shall be faced not only with an accumulated backlog of delayed adjustments—all those businesses which have been kept above water only by continued inflation. Inflation also becomes the active cause of new 'misdirections' of production, i.e., it induces new activities which will continue to be profitable only so long as inflation lasts. Especially when the additional money first becomes available for investment activities, these will be increased to a volume which cannot be maintained once only current savings are available to feed them.

The conception that we can maintain prosperity by keeping final demand always increasing a jump ahead of costs must sooner or later prove an illusion, because costs are not an independent magnitude but are in the long run determined by the expectations of what final demand will be. And to secure 'full employment' even an excess of 'aggregate demand' over 'aggregate costs' may not lastingly be sufficient, since the volume of employment depends largely on the magnitude of investment and beyond a certain point an excessive final demand may act as a deterrent rather than as a stimulus to investment.

I fear that those who believe that we have solved the problem of permanent full employment are in for a serious disillusionment. This is not to say that we need have a major depression. A transition to more stable monetary conditions by gradually slowing down inflation is probably still possible. But it will hardly be possible without a significant decrease of employment of some duration. The difficulty is that in the present state of opinion any noticeable increase of unemployment will at once be met by renewed inflation. Such attempts to cure unemployment by further doses of inflation will probably be temporarily successful and may even succeed several times if the inflationary pressure is massive enough. But this will merely postpone the problem and in the meantime aggravate the inherent instability of the situation.

In a short paper on the twenty years' outlook there is no space to consider the serious but essentially short-term problem of how to get out of a particular inflationary spell without producing a major depression. The long-term problem is how we are to stop the long-term and periodically accelerated inflationary trend which will again and again raise that problem. The essential point is that it must be once more realised that the employment problem is a wage problem and that the Keynesian device of lowering real wages by reducing the value of money when wages have become too high for full employment will work only so long as the workers let themselves be deceived by it. It was an attempt to get round what is called the 'rigidity' of wages which could work for a time but which in the long run has only made this obstacle to a stable monetary system greater than it had been. What is needed is that the responsibility for a wage level which is compatible with a high and stable level of employment should again be squarely placed where it belongs: with the trade unions. The present division of responsibility where each union is concerned only with obtaining the maximum rate of money wages without regard to the effect on employment, and the monetary authorities are expected to supply whatever increases of money income are required to secure full employment at the resulting wage level, must lead to continuous and progressive inflation. We are discovering that by refusing to face the wage problem and temporarily evading the consequences by monetary deception, we have merely made the whole problem much more difficult. The long-run problem remains the restoration of a labour market which will produce wages which are compatible with stable money. This means that the full and exclusive responsibility of the monetary authorities for inflation must once more be recognised. Though it is true that, so long as it is regarded as their duty to supply enough money to secure full employment at any wage level, they have no choice and their role becomes a purely passive one, it is this very conception which is bound to produce continuous inflation. Stable monetary conditions require that the stream of money expenditure is the fixed datum to which prices and wages have to adapt themselves, and not the other way round.

The State of Public Opinion

Such a change of policy as would be required to prevent progressive inflation, and the instability and recurrent crises it is bound to produce, presupposes, however, a change in the still predominant state of opinion. Though a 7 percent Bank rate in the country where they originated and were most consistently practised proclaims loudly the bankruptcy of Keynesian principles, there is yet little sign that they have lost their sway over the generation that grew up in their heyday. But quite apart from this intellectual power they still exercise, they have contributed so much to strengthen the position of one of the politically most powerful elements in the country, that their abandonment is not likely to come without a severe political struggle. The desire to avoid this will probably again and again lead politicians to put off the necessity by resorting once more to the temporary way out which inflation offers as the path of least resistance. It will probably be only when the dangers of this path have become much more obvious than they are now that the fundamental underlying problem of union power will really be faced.

(*Studies in Philosophy, Politics and Economics,* pp. 295–99)

16. Labour Unions and Employment

Professor Hayek makes two major points in this extract from the Constitution of Liberty. *First, it is unwarranted, he says, to identify the interests of union members with the interests of the working class as a whole, since unions are able to obtain higher wage rates for their members only by limiting the supply of unionised labour and thus increasing the supply of* non-*union labour—i.e., by reducing the wage rates of non-union workers.*

Secondly, the separate attempts of each union to raise real wages by raising the money wages of its members would produce unemployment, unless *the monetary authorities inflated the flow of money incomes to compensate for this discoordination; but such an inflation in turn leads to even graver consequences.*

Public policy concerning labour unions has, in little more than a century, moved from one extreme to the other. From a state in which little the unions could do was legal if they were not prohibited altogether, we have now reached a state where they have become uniquely privileged institutions to which the general rules of law do not apply. They have become the only important instance in which governments signally fail in their prime function—the prevention of coercion and violence.

This development has been greatly assisted by the fact that unions were at first able to appeal to the general principles of liberty[1] and then retain the support of the liberals long after all discrimination against them had ceased and they had acquired exceptional privileges. In few other areas are progressives so little willing to consider the reasonableness of any particular measure but generally ask only whether it is 'For or against unions' or, as it is usually put, 'For or against labour'.[2] Yet the briefest glance at the history of the unions should suggest that the reasonable position must lie somewhere between the extremes which mark their evolution.

Changed Character of the Problem

Most people, however, have so little realisation of what has happened that they still support the aspirations of the unions in the belief that they are struggling for 'freedom of association', when this term has in fact lost its meaning and the real issue has become the freedom of the individual to join or not to join a union. The existing confusion is due in part to the rapidity with which the character of the problem

---

[1] Including the most 'orthodox' political economists, who invariably supported freedom of association. See particularly the discussion in J.R. McCulloch, *Treatise on the Circumstances Which Determine the Rate of Wages and the Condition of the Labouring Classes* (London, 1851), pp. 79–89, with its stress on *voluntary* association. For a comprehensive statement of the classical liberal attitude toward the legal problems involved see Ludwig Bamberger, *Die Arbeiterfrage unter dem Gesichtspunkte des Vereinsrechtes* (Stuttgart, 1873).

[2] Characteristic is the description of the 'liberal' attitude to unions in C.W. Mills, *The New Men of Power* (New York: Harcourt Brace, 1948), p. 21:

> 'In many liberal minds there seems to be an undercurrent that whispers: "I will not criticise the unions and their leaders. There I draw the line." This, they must feel, distinguishes them from the bulk of the Republican Party and the right-wing Democrats, this keeps them leftward and socially pure.'

has changed; in many countries voluntary associations of workers had only just become legal when they began to use coercion to force unwilling workers into membership and to keep non-members out of employment. Most people probably still believe that a 'labour dispute' normally means a disagreement about remuneration and the conditions of employment, while as often as not its sole cause is an attempt on the part of the unions to force unwilling workers to join.

The acquisition of privilege by the unions has nowhere been as spectacular as in Britain, where the Trade Disputes Act of 1906 conferred

> upon a trade union a freedom from civil liability for the commission of even the most heinous wrong by the union or its servant, and in short confer[red] upon every trade union a privilege and protection not possessed by any other person or body of persons, whether corporate or incorporate.[3]

---

[3] A.V. Dicey, 'Introduction' to the second edition of his *Law and Opinion* (London: Macmillan, 1914), pp. xlv–xlvi. He continues to say that the law

> makes a trade union a privileged body exempted from the ordinary law of the land. No such privileged body has ever before been deliberately created by an English Parliament [and that] it stimulates among workmen the fatal delusion that workmen should aim at the attainment, not of equality, but of privilege.

Cf. also the comment on the same law thirty years later, by J.A. Schumpeter, *Capitalism, Socialism, and Democracy* (New York: Harper & Row, 1942), p. 321:

> It is difficult, at the present time, to realise how this measure must have struck people who still believed in a state and in a legal system that centred in the institution of private property. For in relaxing the law of conspiracy in respect to peaceful picketing—which practically amounted to legalisation of trade-union action implying the threat of force—and in exempting trade-union funds from liability in action for damages *for torts*—which practically amounted to enacting that trade unions could do no wrong—this measure in fact resigned to the trade unions part of the authority of the state and granted to them a position of privilege which

Similar friendly legislation helped the unions in the United States, where first the Clayton Act of 1914 exempted them from the anti-monopoly provisions of the Sherman Act; the Norris–La Guardia Act of 1932 'went a long way to establish practically complete immunity of labour organisations for torts';[4] and, finally, the Supreme Court in a crucial decision sustained 'the claim of a union to the right to deny participation in the economic world to an employer'.[5] More or less the same situation had gradually come to exist in most European countries by the 1920s, 'less through explicit legislative permission than by the tacit toleration by authorities and courts'.[6] Everywhere the legalisation of unions was interpreted as a legalisation of their main purpose and as recognition of their right to do whatever seemed necessary to achieve this purpose—namely, monopoly. More and more they came to be treated not as a group which was pursuing a legitimate selfish aim and which, like every other interest, must be kept in check by competing interests possessed of equal rights, but as a group whose aim—the exhaustive and comprehensive organisation of all labour—must be supported for the good of the public.[7]

---

the formal extension of the exemption to employers' unions was powerless to affect.

Still more recently the Lord Chief Justice of Northern Ireland said of the same act (Lord MacDermott, *Protection from Power under English Law* [London: Stevens & Sons, 1957], p. 174): 'In short, it put trade unionism in the same privileged position which the Crown enjoyed until ten years ago in respect of wrongful acts committed on its behalf'.

[4] Roscoe Pound, *Legal Immunities of Labor Unions* (Washington, D.C.: American Enterprise Association, 1957), p. 23, reprinted in E.H. Chamberlin, and others, *Labor Unions and Public Policy* (Washington, D.C.: American Enterprise Association, 1958).

[5] Justice Jackson dissenting in *Hunt v. Crumboch,* 325 US 831 (1946).

[6] Ludwig von Mises, *Die Gemeinwirtschaft* (2nd ed.; Jena: Gustav Fischer, 1932), p. 447.

[7] Few liberal sympathisers of the trade unions would dare to express the obvious truth which a courageous woman from within the British labour movement frankly stated, namely, that 'it is in fact the business of a Union to be anti-social; the members would have a just grievance if their officials and committees ceased to put sectional interests

Although flagrant abuses of their powers by the unions have often shocked public opinion in recent times and uncritical pro-union sentiment is on the wane, the public has certainly not yet become aware that the existing legal position is fundamentally wrong and that the whole basis of our free society is gravely threatened by the powers arrogated by the unions. We shall not be concerned here with those criminal abuses of union power that have lately attracted much attention in the United States, although they are not entirely unconnected with the privileges that unions legally enjoy. Our concern will be solely with those powers that unions today generally possess, either with the explicit permission of the law or at least with the tacit toleration of the law-enforcing authorities. Our argument will not be directed against labour unions as such; nor will it be confined to the practices that are now widely recognised as abuses. But we shall direct our attention to some of their powers which are now widely accepted as legitimate, if not as their 'sacred rights'. The case against these is strengthened rather than weakened by the fact that unions have often shown much restraint in exercising them. It is precisely because, in the existing legal situation, unions could do infinitely more harm than they do, and because we owe it to the moderation and good sense of many union leaders that the situation is not much worse, that we cannot afford to allow the present state of affairs to continue.[8]

---

first' (Barbara Wootton, *Freedom under Planning* [London: Allen & Unwin, 1945], p. 97). On the flagrant abuses of union power in the United States, which I shall not further consider here, see Sylvester Petro, *Power Unlimited: The Corruption of Union Leadership* (New York: The Ronald Press Company, 1959).

[8]In this chapter, more than in almost any other, I shall be able to draw upon a body of opinion that is gradually forming among an increasing number of thoughtful students of these matters—men who in background and interest are at least as sympathetic to the true concerns of the workers as those who in the past have been championing the privileges of the unions. See particularly W.H. Hutt, *The Theory of Collective Bargaining* (London: P.S. King, 1930), and *Economists and the Public* (London: Jonathan Cape, 1936); H.C. Simons, 'Some Reflections on Syndicalism', *Journal of Political Economy* LII (1944), reprinted in *Economic Policy for a Free Society* (Chicago: University Chicago Press, 1948); J.T. Dunlop, *Wage Determination under Trade Unions* (New York: Macmillan, 1944); *Economic Institute on Wage Determination and the Economics*

Union Coercion of Fellow Workers

It cannot be stressed enough that the coercion which unions have been permitted to exercise contrary to all principles of freedom under the law is primarily the coercion of fellow workers. Whatever true coercive power unions may be able to wield over employers is a consequence of this primary power of coercing other workers; the coercion of employers would lose most of its objectionable character if unions were deprived of this power to exact unwilling support. Neither the right of voluntary agreement between workers nor even their right to withhold their services in concert is in question. It should be said, however, that the latter—the right to strike—though a normal right, can hardly be regarded as an inalienable right. There are good reasons why in certain employments it should be part of the

---

of Liberalism (Washington, D.C.: Chamber of Commerce of the United States, 1947) (especially the contributions 'Wage Determination as a Part of the General Problem of Monopoly', by Jacob Viner and 'Monopolistic Wage Determination as a Part of the General Problem of Monopoly', by Fritz Machlup); Leo Wolman, *Industry-wide Bargaining* (Irvington-on-Hudson, N.Y.: Foundation for Economic Education, 1948); C.E. Lindblom, *Unions and Capitalism* (New Haven, Conn.: Yale University Press, 1949) (cf. the reviews of this book by A. Director, *University of Chicago Law Review* XVIII [1950]; by J.T. Dunlop in *American Economic Review* XL [1950]; and by Albert Rees in *Journal of Political Economy* LVIII [1950]); *The Impact of the Union,* ed. David McCord Wright (New York: Harcourt Brace, 1951 [especially the contributions 'Some Comments on the Significance of Labor Unions for Economic Policy', by M. Friedman and 'Wage Policy, Employment, and Economic Stability', by G. Haberler]); Fritz Machlup, *The Political Economy of Monopoly* (Baltimore: Johns Hopkins Press, 1952); D.R. Richberg, *Labor Union Monopoly* (Chicago: Henry Regnery, 1957); Sylvester Petro, *The Labor Policy of the Free Society* (New York: The Ronald Press Company, 1957); E.H. Chamberlin, *The Economic Analysis of Labor Power* (1958), P.D. Bradley, *Involuntary Participation in Unionism* (1956), and G.D. Reilly, *State Rights and the Law of Labor Relations* (1955), all three published by the American Enterprise Association (Washington, D.C.) and reprinted together with the pamphlet by Roscoe Pound (*Legal Immunities of Labor Unions*; B.C. Roberts, *Trade Unions in a Free Society* (London: Institute of Economic Affairs, 1959); and John Davenport, 'Labor Unions in the Free Society', *Fortune* (April, 1959), and 'Labor and the Law', *Fortune* (May, 1959). On general wage theory and the limits of the powers of the unions see also J.R. Hicks, *The Theory of Wages* (London: Macmillan, 1932); R. Strigl, *Angewandte Lohntheorie* (Leipzig and Vienna: Franz Deuticke, 1926); and *The Theory of Wage Determination,* ed. J.T. Dunlop (London: Macmillan, 1957).

terms of employment that the worker should renounce this right; i.e., such employments should involve long-term obligations on the part of the workers, and any concerted attempts to break such contracts should be illegal.

It is true that any union effectively controlling all potential workers of a firm or industry can exercise almost unlimited pressure on the employer and that, particularly where a great amount of capital has been invested in specialised equipment, such a union can practically expropriate the owner and command nearly the whole return of his enterprise.[9] The decisive point, however, is that this will never be in the interest of all workers—except in the unlikely case where the total gain from such action is equally shared among them, irrespective of whether they are employed or not—and that, therefore, the union can achieve this only by coercing some workers against their interest to support such a concerted move.

The reason for this is that workers can raise real wages above the level that would prevail on a free market only by limiting the supply, that is, by withholding part of labour. The interest of those who will get employment at the higher wage will therefore always be opposed to the interest of those who, in consequence, will find employment only in the less highly-paid jobs or who will not be employed at all.

The fact that unions will ordinarily first make the employer agree to a certain wage and then see to it that nobody will be employed for less makes little difference. Wage fixing is quite as effective a means as any other of keeping out those who could be employed only at a lower wage. The essential point is that the employer will agree to the wage only when he knows that the union has the power to keep

---

[9] See particularly the works by H.C. Simons and W.H. Hutt cited in the preceding note. Whatever limited validity the old argument about the necessity of 'equalising bargaining power' by the formation of unions may ever have had, has certainly been destroyed by the modern development of the increasing size and specificity of the employers' investment, on the one hand, and the increasing mobility of labour (made possible by the automobile), on the other.

out others.[10] As a general rule, wage fixing (whether by unions or by authority) will make wages higher than they would otherwise be only if they are also higher than the wage at which all willing workers can be employed.

Wage Increases at Expense of Others
Though unions may still often act on a contrary belief, there can now be no doubt that they cannot in the long run increase real wages for all wishing to work above the level that would establish itself in a free market—though they may well push up the level of money wages, with consequences that will occupy us later. Their success in raising real wages beyond that point, if it is to be more than temporary, can benefit only a particular group at the expense of others. It will therefore serve only a sectional interest even when it obtains the support of all. This means that strictly voluntary unions, because their wage policy would not be in the interest of all workers, could not long receive the support of all. Unions that had no power to coerce outsiders would thus not be strong enough to force up wages above the level at which all seeking work could be employed, that is, the level that would establish itself in a truly free market for labour in general.

But, while the real wages of all the employed can be raised by union action only at the price of unemployment, unions in particular industries or crafts may well raise the wages of their members by forcing others to stay in less well-paid occupations. How great a distortion of the wage structure this in fact causes is difficult to say. If one remembers, however, that some unions find it expedient to use violence in order to prevent any influx into their trade and that others are able to charge high premiums for admission (or even to reserve jobs in the trade for children of present members), there can be little doubt that this distortion is considerable. It is important to

---

[10]This must be emphasised especially against the argument of Lindblom in *Unions and Capitalism*.

note that such policies can be employed successfully only in relatively prosperous and highly-paid occupations and that they will therefore result in the exploitation of the relatively poor by the better-off. Even though within the scope of any one union its actions may tend to reduce differences in remuneration, there can be little doubt that, so far as relative wages in major industries and trades are concerned, unions today are largely responsible for an inequality which has no function and is entirely the result of privilege.[11] This means that their activities necessarily reduce the productivity of labour all around and therefore also the general level of real wages; because, if union action succeeds in reducing the number of workers in the highly-paid jobs and in increasing the number of those who have to stay in the less remunerative ones, the result must be that the overall average will be lower. It is, in fact, more than likely that, in countries where unions are very strong, the general level of real wages is lower than it would otherwise be.[12] This is certainly true of most countries of Europe, where union policy is strengthened by the general use of restrictive practices of a 'make-work' character.

If many still accept as an obvious and undeniable fact that the general wage level has risen as fast as it has done because of the efforts of the unions, they do so in spite of these unambiguous conclusions of theoretical analysis—and in spite of empirical evidence to the contrary. Real wages have often risen much faster when unions were weak than when they were strong; furthermore, even the rise in particular trades or industries where labour was not organised has frequently been much faster than in highly organised and equally prosperous

---

[11]Chamberlin, *The Economic Analysis of Labor Power*, pp. 4–5, rightly stresses that 'there can be no doubt that one effect of trade union policy . . . is to diminish still further the real income of the really low income groups, including not only the low income wage receivers but also such other elements of society as "self-employed" and small business men'.

[12]Cf. F. Machlup in these two studies: 'Monopolistic Wage Determination as a Part of the General Problem of Monopoly' and *The Political Economy of Monopoly*.

industries.[13] The common impression to the contrary is due partly to the fact that wage gains, which are today mostly obtained in union negotiations, are for that reason regarded as obtainable only in this manner[14] and even more to the fact that, as we shall presently see, union activity does in fact bring about a continuous rise in money wages exceeding the increase in real wages. Such increase in money wages is possible without producing general unemployment only because it is regularly made ineffective by inflation—indeed, it must be if full employment is to be maintained.

Harmful and Dangerous Activities
If unions have in fact achieved much less by their wage policy than is generally believed, their activities in this field are nevertheless economically very harmful and politically exceedingly dangerous. They are using their power in a manner which tends to make the market system ineffective and which, at the same time, gives them a control of the direction of economic activity that would be dangerous in the hands of government but is intolerable if exercised by a particular group. They do so through their influence on the relative wages of different groups of workers and through their constant upward pressure on the level of money wages, with its inevitable inflationary consequences.

The effect on relative wages is usually greater uniformity and rigidity of wages within any one union-controlled group and greater and non-functional differences in wages between different groups. This is accompanied by a restriction of the mobility of labour, of which the former is either an effect or a cause. We need say no more

---

[13] A conspicuous example of this in recent times is the case of the notoriously unorganised domestic servants whose average annual wages (as pointed out by M. Friedman in D. Wright's *The Impact of the Union,* p. 224) in the United States in 1947 were 2.72 times as high as they had been in 1939, while at the end of the same period the wages of the comprehensively organised steel workers had risen only to 1.98 times the initial level.

[14] Cf. Bradley, *Involuntary Participation in Unionism.*

about the fact that this may benefit particular groups but can only lower the productivity and therefore the incomes of the workers in general. Nor need we stress here the fact that the greater stability of the wages of particular groups which unions may secure is likely to involve greater instability of employment. What is important is that the accidental differences in union power of the different trades and industries will produce not only gross inequalities in remuneration among the workers which have no economic justification but uneconomic disparities in the development of different industries. Socially important industries, such as building, will be greatly hampered in their development and will conspicuously fail to satisfy urgent needs simply because their character offers the unions special opportunities for coercive monopolistic practices.[15] Because unions are most powerful where capital investments are heaviest, they tend to become a deterrent to investment—at present probably second only to taxation. Finally, it is often union monopoly in collusion with enterprise that becomes one of the chief foundations of monopolistic control of the industry concerned.

The chief danger presented by the current development of unionism is that, by establishing effective monopolies in the supply of the different kinds of labour, the unions will prevent competition from acting as an effective regulator of the allocation of all resources. But if competition becomes ineffective as a means of such regulation, some other means will have to be adopted in its place. The only alternative to the market, however, is direction by authority. Such direction clearly cannot be left in the hands of particular unions with sectional interests, nor can it be adequately performed by a unified organisation of all labour, which would thereby become not merely the strongest power in the state but a power completely controlling the state. Unionism as it is now tends, however, to produce that very

---

[15]Cf. S.P. Sobotka, 'Union Influence on Wages: The Construction Industry', *Journal of Political Economy* LXI (1953).

system of overall socialist planning which few unions want and which, indeed, it is in their best interest to avoid.

Acting against Members' Interests
The unions cannot achieve their principal aims unless they obtain complete control of the supply of the type of labour with which they are concerned; and, since it is not in the interest of all workers to submit to such control, some of them must be induced to act against their own interest. This may be done to some extent through merely psychological and moral pressure, encouraging the erroneous belief that the unions benefit all workers. Where they succeed in creating a general feeling that every worker ought, in the interest of his class, to support union action, coercion comes to be accepted as a legitimate means of making a recalcitrant worker do his duty. Here the unions have relied on a most effective tool, namely, the myth that it is due to their efforts that the standard of living of the working class has risen as fast as it has done and that only through their continued efforts will wages continue to increase as fast as possible—a myth in the assiduous cultivation of which the unions have usually been actively assisted by their opponents. A departure from such a condition can only come from a truer insight into the facts, and whether this will be achieved depends on how effectively economists do their job of enlightening public opinion.

But though this kind of moral pressure exerted by the unions may be very powerful, it would scarcely be sufficient to give them the power to do real harm. Union leaders apparently agree with the students of this aspect of unionism that much stronger forms of coercion are needed if the unions are to achieve their aims. It is the techniques of coercion that unions have developed for the purpose of making membership in effect compulsory, what they call their 'organisational activities' (or, in the United States, 'union security'—a curious euphemism) that give them real power. Because the power of truly voluntary unions will be restricted to what are common interests of all workers, they have come to direct their chief efforts to the forcing of dissenters to obey their will.

They could never have been successful in this without the support of a misguided public opinion and the active aid of government. Unfortunately, they have to a large extent succeeded in persuading the public that complete unionisation is not only legitimate but important to public policy. To say that the workers have a right to form unions, however, is not to say that the unions have a right to exist independently of the will of the individual workers. Far from being a public calamity, it would indeed be a highly desirable state of affairs if the workers should not feel it necessary to form unions. Yet the fact that it is a natural aim of the unions to induce all workers to join them has been so interpreted as to mean that the unions ought to be entitled to do whatever seems necessary to achieve this aim. Similarly, the fact that it is legitimate for unions to try to secure higher wages has been interpreted to mean that they must also be allowed to do whatever seems necessary to succeed in their effort. In particular, because striking has been accepted as a legitimate weapon of unions, it has come to be believed that they must be allowed to do whatever seems necessary to make a strike successful. In general, the legalisation of unions has come to mean that whatever methods they regard as indispensable for their purposes are also to be treated as legal.

The present coercive powers of unions thus rest chiefly on the use of methods which would not be tolerated for any other purpose and which are opposed to the protection of the individual's private sphere. In the first place, the unions rely—to a much greater extent than is commonly recognised—on the use of the picket line as an instrument of intimidation. That even so-called 'peaceful' picketing in numbers is severely coercive and the condoning of it constitutes a privilege conceded because of its presumed legitimate aim is shown by the fact that it can be and is used by persons who themselves are not workers to force others to form a union which they will control, and that it can also be used for purely political purposes or to give vent to animosity against an unpopular person. The aura of legitimacy conferred upon it because the aims are often approved cannot alter the fact that it represents a kind of organised pressure upon individuals which in a free society no private agency should be permitted to exercise.

Next to the toleration of picketing, the chief factor which enables unions to coerce individual workers is the sanction by both legislation and jurisdiction of the closed or union shop and its varieties. These constitute contracts in restraint of trade, and only their exemption from the ordinary rules of law has made them legitimate objects of the 'organisational activities' of the unions. Legislation has frequently gone so far as to require not only that a contract concluded by the representatives of the majority of the workers of a plant or industry be available to any worker who wishes to take advantage of it, but that it apply to all employees, even if they should individually wish and be able to obtain a different combination of advantages.[16] We must also regard as inadmissible methods of coercion all secondary strikes and boycotts which are used not as an instrument of wage bargaining but solely as a means of forcing other workers to fall in with union policies.

Most of these coercive tactics of the unions can be practised, moreover, only because the law has exempted groups of workers from the ordinary responsibility of joint action, either by allowing them to avoid formal incorporation or by explicitly exempting their organisations from the general rules applying to corporate bodies. There is no need to consider separately various other aspects of contemporary union policies such as, to mention one, industry-wide or

---

[16] It would be difficult to exaggerate the extent to which unions prevent the experimentation with, and gradual introduction of, new arrangements that might be in the mutual interest of employers and employees. For example, it is not at all unlikely that in some industries it would be in the interest of both to agree on 'guaranteed annual wages' if unions permitted individuals to make a sacrifice in the amount of wages in return for a greater degree of security.

nation-wide bargaining. Their practicability rests on the practices already mentioned, and they would almost certainly disappear if the basic coercive power of the unions were removed.[17]

A Non-coercive Role

It can hardly be denied that raising wages by the use of coercion is today the main aim of unions. Even if this were their sole aim, legal prohibition of unions would, however, not be justifiable. In a free society much that is undesirable has to be tolerated if it cannot be prevented without discriminatory legislation. But the control of wages is even now not the only function of the unions; and they are undoubtedly capable of rendering services which are not only unobjectionable but definitely useful. If their only purpose were to force up wages by coercive action, they would probably disappear if deprived of coercive power. But unions have other useful functions to perform, and, though it would be contrary to all our principles even to consider the possibility of prohibiting them altogether, it is desirable to show explicitly why there is no economic ground for such action and why, as truly voluntary and non-coercive organizations,

---

[17]To illustrate the nature of much contemporary wage bargaining in the United States, E.H. Chamberlin, in *The Economic Analysis of Labor Power*, uses an analogy which I cannot better:

> Some perspective may be had on what is involved by imagining an application of the techniques of the labour market in some other field. If A is bargaining with B over the sale of his house, and if A were given the privileges of a modern labour union, he would be able (1) to conspire with all other owners of houses not to make any alternative offers to B, using violence or the threat of violence if necessary to prevent them, (2) to deprive B himself of access to any alternative offers, (3) to surround the house of B and cut off all deliveries of food (except by parcel post), (4) to stop all movement from B's house, so that if he were for instance a doctor he could not sell his services and make a living, and (5) to institute a boycott of B's business. All of these privileges, if he were capable of carrying them out, would no doubt strengthen A's position. But they would not be regarded by anyone as part of 'bargaining'—unless A were a labour union.

they may have important services to render. It is in fact more than probable that unions will fully develop their potential usefulness only after they have been diverted from their present anti-social aims by an effective prevention of the use of coercion.[18]

Unions without coercive powers would probably play a useful and important role even in the process of wage determination. In the first place, there is often a choice to be made between wage increases, on the one hand, and, on the other, alternative benefits which the employer could provide at the same cost but which he can provide only if all or most of the workers are willing to accept them in preference to additional pay. There is also the fact that the relative position of the individual on the wage scale is often nearly as important to him as his absolute position. In any hierarchical organisation it is important that the differentials between the remuneration for the different jobs and the rules of promotion are felt to be just by the majority.[19] The most effective way of securing consent is probably to have the general scheme agreed to in collective negotiations in which all the different interests are represented. Even from the employer's point of view it would be difficult to conceive of any other way of reconciling all the different considerations that in a large organisation have to be taken into account in arriving at a satisfactory wage structure. An agreed set of standard terms, available to all who wish to take advantage of

---

[18] Cf. Petro, *The Labor Policy of the Free Society*, p. 51:

> Unions can and do serve useful purposes, and they have only barely scratched the surface of their potential utility to employees. When they really get to work on the job of serving employees instead of making such bad names for themselves as they do in coercing and abusing employers, they will have much less difficulty than they presently have in securing and keeping new members. As matters now stand, union insistence upon the closed shop amounts to an admission that unions are really not performing their functions very well.

[19] Cf. C.I. Barnard, 'Functions and Pathology of Status Systems in Formal Organizations', in *Industry and Society,* ed. W.F. Whyte (New York: McGraw-Hill 1946), reprinted in Barnard's *Organization and Management* (Cambridge, Mass.: Harvard University Press, 1949).

them, though not excluding special arrangements in individual cases, seems to be required by the needs of large-scale organisations.

The same is true to an even greater extent of all the general problems relating to conditions of work other than individual remuneration, those problems which truly concern all employees and which, in the mutual interest of workers and employers, should be regulated in a manner that takes account of as many desires as possible. A large organisation must in a great measure be governed by rules, and such rules are likely to operate most effectively if drawn up with the participation of the workers.[20] Because a contract between employers and employees regulates not only relations between them but also relations between the various groups of employees, it is often expedient to give it the character of a multilateral agreement and to provide in certain respects, as in grievance procedure, for a degree of self-government among the employees.

There is, finally, the oldest and most beneficial activity of the unions, in which as 'friendly societies' they undertake to assist members in providing against the peculiar risks of their trade. This is a function which must in every respect be regarded as a highly desirable form of self-help, albeit one which is gradually being taken over by the state. We shall leave the question open, however, as to whether any of the above arguments justify unions of a larger scale than that of the plant or corporation.

An entirely different matter, which we can mention here only in passing, is the claim of unions to participation in the conduct of business. Under the name of 'industrial democracy' or, more recently, under that of 'codetermination', this has acquired considerable popularity, especially in Germany and to a lesser degree in Britain.

---

[20]Cf. Sumner Slichter, *Trade Unions in a Free Society* (Cambridge, Mass: Harvard University Press, 1947), p. 12, where it is argued that such rules 'introduce into industry the equivalent of civil rights, and they greatly enlarge the range of human activities which are governed by rule of law rather than by whim or caprice.' See also A.W. Gouldner, *Patterns of Industrial Bureaucracy* (Glencoe, Ill.: The Free Press, 1954), especially the discussion of 'rule by rule'.

It represents a curious recrudescence of the ideas of the syndicalist branch of nineteenth-century socialism, the least thought-out and most impractical form of that doctrine. Though these ideas have a certain superficial appeal, they reveal inherent contradictions when examined. A plant or industry cannot be conducted in the interest of some permanent distinct body of workers if it is at the same time to serve the interests of the consumers. Moreover, effective participation in the direction of an enterprise is a full-time job, and anybody so engaged soon ceases to have the outlook and interest of an employee. It is not only from the point of view of the employers, therefore, that such a plan should be rejected; there are very good reasons why in the United States union leaders have emphatically refused to assume any responsibility in the conduct of business. For a fuller examination of this problem we must, however, refer the reader to the careful studies, now available, of all its implications.[21]

Minor Changes in the Law

Though it may be impossible to protect the individual against all union coercion so long as general opinion regards it as legitimate, most students of the subject agree that comparatively few and, as they may seem at first, minor changes in law and jurisdiction would suffice to produce far-reaching and probably decisive changes in the existing situation.[22] The mere withdrawal of the special privileges either explicitly granted to the unions or arrogated by them with the toleration of the courts would seem enough to deprive them of the more serious coercive powers which they now exercise and to

---

[21] See particularly Franz Böhm, 'Das wirtschaftliche Mitbestimmungsrecht der Arbeiter im Betrieb', *Ordo* IV (1951); and Götz Briefs, *Zwischen Kapitalismus und Syndikalismus* (Bern: Francke, 1952).

[22] See the essays 'Wage Determination as a Part of the General Problem of Monopoly', by Viner and 'Wage Policy, Employment, and Economic Stability', by Haberler; 'Some Comments on the Significance of Labor Unions for Economic Policy', by Friedman; and the book *The Labor Policy of the Free Society* by Petro.

channel their legitimate selfish interests so that they would be socially beneficial.

The essential requirement is that true freedom of association be assured and that coercion be treated as equally illegitimate whether employed for or against organisation, by the employer or by the employees. The principle that the end does not justify the means and that the aims of the unions do not justify their exemption from the general rules of law should be strictly applied. Today this means, in the first place, that all picketing in numbers should be prohibited, since it is not only the chief and regular cause of violence but even in its most peaceful forms is a means of coercion. Next, the unions should not be permitted to keep non-members out of any employment. This means that closed- and union-shop contracts (including such varieties as the 'maintenance of membership' and 'preferential hiring' clauses) must be treated as contracts in restraint of trade and denied the protection of the law. They differ in no respect from the 'yellow-dog contract' which prohibits the individual worker from joining a union and which is commonly prohibited by the law.

The invalidating of all such contracts would, by removing the chief objects of secondary strikes and boycotts, make these and similar forms of pressure largely ineffective. It would be necessary, however, also to rescind all legal provisions which make contracts concluded with the representatives of the majority of workers of a plant or industry binding on all employees and to deprive all organised groups of any right of concluding contracts binding on men who have not voluntarily delegated this authority to them.[23] Finally, the responsibility for organised and concerted action in conflict with contractual obligations or the general law must be firmly placed on those in whose hands the decision lies, irrespective of the particular form of organized action adopted.

---

[23]Such contracts binding on third parties are equally as objectionable in this field as is the forcing of price-maintenance agreements on non-signers by 'fair-trade' laws.

It would not be a valid objection to maintain that any legislation making certain types of contracts invalid would be contrary to the principle of freedom of contract. We have seen before (in Chap. xv) that this principle can never mean that all contracts will be legally binding and enforceable. It means merely that all contracts must be judged according to the same general rules and that no authority should be given discretionary power to allow or disallow particular contracts. Among the contracts to which the law ought to deny validity are contracts in restraint of trade. Closed- and union-shop contracts fall clearly into this category. If legislation, jurisdiction, and the tolerance of executive agencies had not created privileges for the unions, the need for special legislation concerning them would probably not have arisen in common-law countries. That there is such a need is a matter for regret, and the believer in liberty will regard any legislation of this kind with misgivings. But, once special privileges have become part of the law of the land, they can be removed only by special legislation. Though there ought to be no need for special 'right-to-work laws', it is difficult to deny that the situation created in the United States by legislation and by the decisions of the Supreme Court may make special legislation the only practicable way of restoring the principles of freedom.[24]

The specific measures which would be required in any given country to reinstate the principles of free association in the field of labour will depend on the situation created by its individual development. The situation in the United States is of special interest, for here legislation and the decisions of the Supreme Court have

---

[24] Such legislation, to be consistent with our principles, should not go beyond declaring certain contracts invalid, which is sufficient for removing all pretext for action to obtain them. It should not, as the title of the 'right-to-work laws' may suggest, give individuals a claim to a particular job, or even (as some of the laws in force in certain American states do) confer a right to damages for having been denied a particular job, when the denial is not illegal on other grounds. The objections against such provisions are the same as those which apply to 'fair employment practices' laws.

probably gone further than elsewhere[25] in legalising union coercion and very far in conferring discretionary and essentially irresponsible powers on administrative authority. But for further details we must refer the reader to the important study by Professor Petro on *The Labor Policy of the Free Society*,[26] in which the reforms required are fully described.

Though all the changes needed to restrain the harmful powers of the unions involve no more than that they be made to submit to the same general principles of law that apply to everybody else, there can be no doubt that the existing unions will resist them with all their power. They know that the achievement of what they at present desire depends on that very coercive power which will have to be restrained if a free society is to be preserved. Yet the situation is not hopeless. There are developments under way which sooner or later will prove to the unions that the existing state cannot last. They will find that, of the alternative courses of further development open to them, submitting to the general principle that prevents all coercion will be greatly preferable in the long run to continuing their present policy; for the latter is bound to lead to one of two unfortunate consequences.

Responsibility for Unemployment
While labour unions cannot in the long run substantially alter the level of real wages that all workers can earn and are, in fact, more likely to lower than to raise them, the same is not true of the level of money wages. With respect to them, the effect of union action will depend on the principles governing monetary policy. What with the doctrines that are now widely accepted and the policies accordingly expected from the monetary authorities, there can be little doubt that

---

[25] See A. Lenhoff, 'The Problem of Compulsory Unionism in Europe', *American Journal of Comparative Law* V (1956).

[26] See Petro, *Power Unlimited: The Corruption of Union Leadership,* esp. pp. 235ff. and 282.

current union policies must lead to continuous and progressive inflation. The chief reason for this is that the dominant 'full-employment' doctrines explicitly relieve the unions of the responsibility for any unemployment and place the duty of preserving full employment on the monetary and fiscal authorities. The only way in which the latter can prevent union policy from producing unemployment is, however, to counter through inflation whatever excessive rises in real wages unions tend to cause.

In order to understand the situation into which we have been led, it will be necessary to take a brief look at the intellectual sources of the full-employment policy of the 'Keynesian' type. The development of Lord Keynes's theories started from the correct insight that the regular cause of extensive unemployment is real wages that are too high. The next step consisted in the proposition that a direct lowering of money wages could be brought about only by a struggle so painful and prolonged that it could not be contemplated. Hence he concluded that real wages must be lowered by the process of lowering the value of money. This is really the reasoning underlying the whole 'full-employment' policy, now so widely accepted.[27] If labour insists on a level of money wages too high to allow of full employment, the supply of money must be so increased as to raise prices to a level where the real value of the prevailing money wages is no longer greater than the productivity of the workers seeking employment. In practice, this necessarily means that each separate union, in its attempt to overtake the value of money, will never cease to insist on further increases in money wages and that the aggregate effort of the unions will thus bring about progressive inflation.

This would follow even if individual unions did no more than prevent any reduction in the money wages of any particular group. Where unions make such wage reductions impracticable and wages

---

[27] See the articles by G. Haberler and myself in *Problems of United States Economic Development,* ed. by the Committee for Economic Development, Vol. I (New York, 1958).

have generally become, as the economists put it, 'rigid downward', all the changes in relative wages of the different groups made necessary by the constantly changing conditions must be brought about by raising all money wages except those of the group whose relative real wages must fall. Moreover, the general rise in money wages and the resulting increase in the cost of living will generally lead to attempts, even on the part of the latter group, to push up money wages, and several rounds of successive wage increases will be required before any readjustment of relative wages is produced. Since the need for adjustment of relative wages occurs all the time, this process alone produces the wage-price spiral that has prevailed since the second World War, that is, since full-employment policies became generally accepted.[28]

The process is sometimes described as though wage increases directly produced inflation. This is not correct. If the supply of money and credit were not expanded, the wage increases would rapidly lead to unemployment. But under the influence of a doctrine that represents it as the duty of the monetary authorities to provide enough money to secure full employment at any given wage level, it is politically inevitable that each round of wage increases should lead to further inflation.[29] Or it is inevitable until the rise of prices

---

[28] Cf. Arthur J Brown, *The Great Inflation, 1939–1951* (London: Oxford University Press, 1955).

[29] See J.R. Hicks, 'Economic Foundations of Wage Policy', *Economic Journal* LXV (1955), esp. p. 391:

> The world we now live in is one in which the monetary system has become relatively elastic, so that it can accommodate itself to changes in wages, rather than the other way about. Instead of actual wages having to adjust themselves to an equilibrium level, monetary policy adjusts the equilibrium level of money wages so as to make it conform to the actual level. It is hardly an exaggeration to say that instead of being on a Gold Standard, we are on a Labour Standard.

But see also the same author's later article, 'The Instability of Wages', *Three Banks Review*, no. 31 (September, 1956).

becomes sufficiently marked and prolonged to cause serious public alarm. Efforts will then be made to apply the monetary brakes. But, because by that time the economy will have become geared to the expectation of further inflation and much of the existing employment will depend on continued monetary expansion, the attempt to stop it will rapidly produce substantial unemployment. This will bring a renewed and irresistible pressure for more inflation. And, with ever bigger doses of inflation, it may be possible for quite a long time to prevent the appearance of the unemployment which the wage pressure would otherwise cause. To the public at large it will seem as if progressive inflation were the direct consequence of union wage policy rather than of an attempt to cure its consequences.

Though this race between wages and inflation is likely to go on for some time, it cannot go on indefinitely without people coming to realise that it must somehow be stopped. A monetary policy that would break the coercive powers of the unions by producing extensive and protracted unemployment must be excluded, for it would be politically and socially fatal. But if we do not succeed in time in curbing union power at its source, the unions will soon be faced with a demand for measures that will be much more distasteful to the individual workers, if not the union leaders, than the submission of the unions to the rule of law: the clamour will soon be either for the fixing of wages by government or for the complete abolition of the unions.

Progression to Central Control

In the field of labour, as in any other field, the elimination of the market as a steering mechanism would necessitate the replacement of it by a system of administrative direction. In order to approach even remotely the ordering function of the market, such direction would have to coordinate the whole economy and therefore, in the last resort, have to come from a single central authority. And though such an authority might at first concern itself only with the allocation and remuneration of labour, its policy would necessarily lead to the transformation of the whole of society into a centrally planned and administered system, with all its economic and political consequences.

In those countries in which inflationary tendencies have operated for some time, we can observe increasingly frequent demands for an 'overall wage policy'. In the countries where these tendencies have been most pronounced, notably in Great Britain, it appears to have become accepted doctrine among the intellectual leaders of the Left that wages should generally be determined by a 'unified policy', which ultimately means that government must do the determining.[30] If the market were thus irretrievably deprived of its function, there would be no efficient way of distributing labour throughout the industries, regions, and trades, other than having wages determined by authority. Step by step, through setting up an official conciliation and arbitration machinery with compulsory powers, and through the creation of wage boards, we are moving towards a situation in which wages will be determined by what must be essentially arbitrary decisions of authority.

All this is no more than the inevitable outcome of the present policies of labour unions, who are led by the desire to see wages determined by some conception of 'justice' rather than by the forces of the market. But in no workable system could any group of people be allowed to enforce by the threat of violence what it believes it should have. And when not merely a few privileged groups but most of the important sections of

---

[30]See W. Beveridge, *Full Employment in a Free Society* (London: George Allen & Unwin, 1944); M. Joseph and N. Kaldor, *Economic Reconstruction after the War* (handbooks published for the Association for Education in Citizenship [London, n.d.]); Barbara Wootton, *The Social Foundations of Wage Policy* (London: George Allen & Unwin, 1955); and, on the present state of the discussion, D.T. Jack, 'Is a Wage Policy Desirable and Practicable?', *Economic Journal* LXVII (1957). It seems that some of the supporters of this development imagine that this wage policy will be conducted by 'labour', which presumably means by joint action of all unions. This seems neither a probable nor a practicable arrangement. Many groups of workers would rightly object to their relative wages being determined by a majority vote of all workers, and a government permitting such an arrangement would in effect transfer all control of economic policy to the labour unions.

labour have become effectively organised for coercive action, to allow each to act independently would not only produce the opposite of justice but result in economic chaos. When we can no longer depend on the impersonal determination of wages by the market, the only way we can retain a viable economic system is to have them determined authoritatively by government. Such determination must be arbitrary, because there are no objective standards of justice that could be applied.[31] As is true of all other prices or services, the wage rates that are compatible with an open opportunity for all to seek employment do not correspond to any assessable merit or any independent standard of justice but must depend on conditions which nobody can control.

Once government undertakes to determine the whole wage structure and is thereby forced to control employment and production, there will be a far greater destruction of the present powers of the unions than their submission to the rule of equal law would involve. Under such a system the unions will have only the choice between becoming the willing instrument of governmental policy and being incorporated into the machinery of government, on the one hand, and being totally abolished, on the other. The former alternative is

---

[31] See, e.g., Barbara Wootton, *Freedom under Planning*, p. 101:

> The continual use of terms like 'fair', however, is quite subjective: no commonly accepted ethical pattern can be implied. The wretched arbitrator, who is charged with the duty of acting 'fairly and impartially', is thus required to show these qualities in circumstances in which they have no meaning; for there can be no such thing as fairness or impartiality except in terms of an accepted code. No one can be impartial in a vacuum. One can only umpire at cricket because there are rules, or at a boxing match so long as certain blows, like those below the belt, are forbidden. Where, therefore, as in wage determinations, there are no rules and no code, the only possible interpretation of impartiality is conservatism.

Also Kenneth F. Walker, *Industrial Relations in Australia* (Cambridge, Mass.: Harvard University Press, 1956), p. 362: 'Industrial tribunals, in contrast with ordinary courts, are called upon to decide issues upon which there is not only no defined law, but not even any commonly accepted standards of fairness or justice.' Cf. also Gertrud Williams [Lady Williams], 'The Myth of "Fair" Wages', *Economic Journal* LXVI (1956).

more likely to be chosen, since it would enable the existing union bureaucracy to retain their position and some of their personal power. But to the workers it would mean complete subjection to the control by a corporative state. The situation in most countries leaves us no choice but to await some such outcome or to retrace our steps. The present position of the unions cannot last, for they can function only in a market economy which they are doing their best to destroy.

'Unassailable' Union Powers

The problem of labour unions constitutes both a good test of our principles and an instructive illustration of the consequences if they are infringed. Having failed in their duty of preventing private coercion, governments are now driven everywhere to exceed their proper function in order to correct the results of that failure and are thereby led into tasks which they can perform only by being as arbitrary as the unions. So long as the powers that the unions have been allowed to acquire are regarded as unassailable, there is no way to correct the harm done by them but to give the state even greater arbitrary power of coercion. We are indeed already experiencing a pronounced decline of the rule of law in the field of labour.[32] Yet all that is really needed to remedy the situation is a return to the principles of the rule of law and to their consistent application by legislative and executive authorities.

---

[32] See Petro, *The Labor Policy of the Free Society,* pp. 262ff., esp. p. 264: 'I shall show in this chapter that the rule of law does not exist in labour relations; that there a man is *entitled* in only exceptional cases to a day in court, no matter how unlawfully he has been harmed'; and p. 272:

> Congress has given the NLRB [National Labor Relations Board] and its General Counsel arbitrary power to deny an injured person a hearing, Congress has closed the federal courts to persons injured by conduct forbidden under federal law. Congress did not, however, prevent unlawfully harmed persons from seeking whatever remedies they might find in state courts. That blow to the ideal that every man is entitled to his day in court was struck by the Supreme Court.

This path is still blocked, however, by the most fatuous of all fashionable arguments, namely, that 'we cannot turn the clock back'. One cannot help wondering whether those who habitually use this cliché are aware that it expresses the fatalistic belief that we cannot learn from our mistakes, the most abject admission that we are incapable of using our intelligence. I doubt whether anybody who takes a long-range view believes that there is another satisfactory solution which the majority would deliberately choose if they fully understood where the present developments were leading. There are some signs that farsighted union leaders are also beginning to recognise that, unless we are to resign ourselves to the progressive extinction of freedom, we must reverse that trend and resolve to restore the rule of law and that, in order to save what is valuable in their movement, they must abandon the illusions which have guided it for so long.[33]

Nothing less than a rededication of current policy to principles already abandoned will enable us to avert the threatening danger to freedom. What is required is a change in economic policy, for in the present situation the tactical decisions which will seem to be required by the short-term needs of government in successive emergencies will merely lead us further into the thicket of arbitrary controls. The cumulative effects of those palliatives which the pursuit of contradictory aims makes necessary must prove strategically fatal. As is true of all problems of economic policy, the problem of labour unions cannot be satisfactorily solved by *ad hoc* decisions on particular

---

[33]The Chairman of the English Trade Union Congress, Mr. Charles Geddes, was reported in 1955 to have said:

> I do not believe that the trade union movement of Great Britain can live for very much longer on the basis of compulsion. Must people belong to us or starve, whether they like our policies or not? No. I believe the trade union card is an honour to be conferred, not a badge which signifies that you have got to do something, whether you like it or not. We want the right to exclude people from our union if necessary and we cannot do that on the basis of 'Belong or starve'.

questions but only by the consistent application of a principle that is uniformly adhered to in all fields. There is only one such principle that can preserve a free society: namely, the strict prevention of all coercion except in the enforcement of general abstract rules equally applicable to all.

(*The Constitution of Liberty*, extracts from Chap. 18)

17. (a) Inflation—A Short-term Expedient
(b) Inflation—The Deceit is Short-lived

In the first of these two extracts, Professor Hayek points out that one effect of inflation in its initial stages is to keep afloat businesses that would otherwise suffer losses. But as inflation proceeds and comes to be expected, costs are bid up in anticipation, profits shrink back to non-*inflationary levels (in real terms), and* apparently *deflationary symptoms begin to appear.*

In the second extract he outlines a non-inflationary criterion for monetary stability in line with currently *unchangeable historical circumstances, viz. maintaining the stability of a comprehensive price index. Given the change in union wage-rate policy outlined in earlier extracts, such a monetary policy would also produce stability in total employment.*

Professor Hayek emphasises two social dangers of inflation. First, by destroying the value of savings and of fixed incomes it creates the problem of poverty in old age, as well as a dangerous gap between the wealthy minority and the propertyless majority. Second, it reinforces the disinclination to take long-term effects into account when determining policy.

17. (a) *Inflation—A Short-term Expedient*
Although there are a few people who deliberately advocate a continuous upward movement of prices, the chief source of the existing inflationary bias is the general belief that deflation, the opposite of inflation, is so much more to be feared that, in order to keep on the safe side, a persistent error in the direction of inflation is preferable. But, as we

do not know how to keep prices completely stable and can achieve stability only by correcting any small movement in either direction, the determination to avoid deflation at any cost must result in cumulative inflation. Also, the fact that inflation and deflation will often be local or sectional phenomena which must occur necessarily as part of the mechanism redistributing the resources of the economy means that attempts to prevent any deflation affecting a major area of the economy must result in overall inflation.

Inflation Similar to Drug-taking
It is, however, rather doubtful whether, from a long-term point of view, deflation is really more harmful than inflation. Indeed, there is a sense in which inflation is infinitely more dangerous and needs to be more carefully guarded against. Of the two errors, it is the one much more likely to be committed. The reason for this is that moderate inflation is generally pleasant while it proceeds, whereas deflation is immediately and acutely painful.[34] There is little need to take precautions against any practice the bad effects of which will be immediately and strongly felt; but there is need for precautions wherever action which is immediately pleasant or relieves temporary difficulties involves much greater harm that will be felt only later. There is, indeed, more than a mere superficial similarity between inflation and drug-taking, a comparison which has often been made.

Inflation and deflation both produce their peculiar effects by causing unexpected price changes, and both are bound to disappoint expectations twice. The first time is when prices prove to be higher or lower than they were expected to be and the second when, as must sooner or later happen, these price changes come to be expected and cease to have the effect which their unforeseen occurrence had. The difference between inflation and deflation is that, with the former, the pleasant surprise comes first and the reaction later, while, with the latter, the first effect on business is depressing. The effects of both,

---

[34]Cf. W. Röpke, *Welfare, Freedom, and Inflation* (London: Pall Mall Press, 1957).

however, are self-reversing. For a time the forces which bring about either tend to feed on themselves, and the period during which prices move faster than expected may thus be prolonged. But unless price movements continue in the same direction at an ever accelerating rate, expectations must catch up with them. As soon as this happens, the character of the effects changes.

Inflation at first merely produces conditions in which more people make profits and in which profits are generally larger than usual. Almost everything succeeds, there are hardly any failures. The fact that profits again and again prove to be greater than had been expected and that an unusual number of ventures turn out to be successful produces a general atmosphere favourable to risk-taking. Even those who would have been driven out of business without the windfalls caused by the unexpected general rise in prices are able to hold on and to keep their employees in the expectation that they will soon share in the general prosperity. This situation will last, however, only until people begin to expect prices to continue to rise at the same rate. Once they begin to count on prices being so many percent higher in so many months' time, they will bid up the prices of the factors of production which determine the costs to a level corresponding to the future prices they expect. If prices then rise no more than had been expected, profits will return to normal, and the proportion of those making a profit also will fall; and since, during the period of exceptionally large profits, many have held on who would otherwise have been forced to change the direction of their efforts, a higher proportion than usual will suffer losses.

The stimulating effect of inflation will thus operate only so long as it has not been foreseen; as soon as it comes to be foreseen, only its continuation at an increased rate will maintain the same degree of prosperity. If in such a situation prices rose less than expected, the effect would be the same as that of unforeseen deflation. Even if they rose only as much as was generally expected, this would no longer provide the exceptional stimulus but would lay bare the whole backlog of adjustments that had been postponed while the temporary stimulus lasted. In order for inflation to retain its initial stimulating effect, it would have to continue at a rate always faster than expected.

Accelerating Inflation

We cannot consider here all the complications which make it impossible for adaptations to an expected change in prices ever to become perfect, and especially for long-term and short-term expectations to become equally adjusted; nor can we go into the different effects on current production and on investment which are so important in any full examination of industrial fluctuations. It is enough for our purpose to know that the stimulating effects of inflation must cease to operate unless its rate is progressively accelerated and that, as it proceeds, certain unfavourable consequences of the fact that complete adaptation is impossible become more and more serious. The most important of these is that the methods of accounting on which all business decisions rest make sense only so long as the value of money is tolerably stable. With prices rising at an accelerating rate, the techniques of capital and cost accounting that provide the basis for all business planning would soon lose all meaning. Real costs, profits, or income would soon cease to be ascertainable by any conventional or generally acceptable method. And, with the principles of taxation being what they are, more and more would be taken in taxes as profits that in fact should be reinvested merely to maintain capital.

Inflation thus can never be more than a temporary fillip, and even this beneficial effect can last only as long as somebody continues to be cheated and the expectations of some people unnecessarily disappointed. Its stimulus is due to the errors which it produces. It is particularly dangerous because the harmful after-effects of even small doses of inflation can be staved off only by larger doses of inflation. Once it has continued for some time, even the prevention of further acceleration will create a situation in which it will be very difficult to avoid a spontaneous deflation. Once certain activities that have become extended can be maintained only by continued inflation, their simultaneous discontinuation, may well produce that vicious and rightly feared process in which the decline of some incomes leads to the decline of other incomes, and so forth. From what we know, it still seems probable that we should be able to prevent serious depressions by preventing the inflations which regularly precede them, but that there is little we can do to cure them, once they have set in. The time to worry about depressions is, unfortunately, when they are furthest from the minds of most people.

The Path of Least Resistance

The manner in which inflation operates explains why it is so difficult to resist when policy mainly concerns itself with particular situations rather than with general conditions and with short-term rather than with long-term problems. It is usually the easy way out of any temporary difficulties for both government and private business—the path of least resistance and sometimes also the easiest way to help the economy get over all the obstacles that government policy has placed in its way.[35] It is the inevitable result of a policy which regards all the other decisions as data to which the supply of money must be adapted so that the damage done by other measures will be as little noticed as possible. In the long run, however, such a policy makes governments the captives of their own earlier decisions, which often force them to adopt measures that they know to be harmful. It is no accident that the author whose views, perhaps mistakenly interpreted, have given more encouragement to these inflationary propensities than any other man's is also responsible for the fundamentally anti-liberal

---

[35]Cf. my essay 'Full Employment, Planning, and Inflation', *Review of the Institute of Public Affairs* IV (Melbourne, Victoria, Australia, 1950); and the German version in *Vollbeschäftigung, Inflation und Planwirtschaft,* ed. A. Hunold (Zurich, 1951); and F.A. Lutz, 'Inflationsgefahr und Konjunkturpolitik', *Schweizerische Zeitschrift fur Volkswirtschaft und Statistik* XCIII (1957), and 'Cost- and Demand-Induced Inflation', *Banca Nazionale de Lavoro Quarterly Review* XLIV (1958).

aphorism, 'in the long run we are all dead'.[36] The inflationary bias of our day is largely the result of the prevalence of the short-term view, which in turn stems from the great difficulty of recognising the more remote consequences of current measures, and from the inevitable preoccupation of practical men, and particularly politicians, with the immediate problems and the achievement of near goals.

Because inflation is psychologically and politically so much more difficult to prevent than deflation and because it is, at the same time, technically so much more easily prevented, the economist should always stress the dangers of inflation. As soon as deflation makes itself felt, there will be immediate attempts to combat it—often when it is only a local and necessary process that should not be prevented. There is more danger in untimely fears of deflation than in the possibility of our not taking necessary counter-measures. While nobody is likely to mistake local or sectional prosperity for inflation, people often demand wholly inappropriate monetary counter-measures when there is a local or sectional depression.

These considerations would seem to suggest that, on balance, probably some mechanical rule which aims at what is desirable in the long run and ties the hands of authority in its short-term decisions is likely to produce a better monetary policy than principles which give to the authorities more power and discretion and thereby make them more subject to both political pressure and their own inclination to overestimate the urgency of the circumstances of the moment. This, however, raises issues which we must approach more systematically.

17. (b) Inflation—The Deceit is Short-lived

I certainly have no wish to weaken the case for any arrangement that will force the authorities to do the right thing. The case for such a mechanism becomes stronger as the likelihood of the monetary policy's being affected by considerations of public finance becomes greater; but it would weaken, rather than strengthen, the argument if we

---

[36]J.M. Keynes, *A Tract on Monetary Reform* (London: Macmillan, 1923), p. 80.

exaggerated what can be achieved by it. It is probably undeniable that, though we can limit discretion in this field, we never can eliminate it; in consequence, what can be done within the unavoidable range of discretion not only is very important but is likely in practice to determine even whether or not the mechanism will ever be allowed to operate.

Limited Central Bank Influence
There is one basic dilemma, which all central banks face, which makes it inevitable that their policy must involve much discretion. A central bank can exercise only an indirect and therefore limited control over all the circulating media. Its power is based chiefly on the threat of not supplying cash when it is needed. Yet at the same time it is considered to be its duty never to refuse to supply this cash at a price when needed. It is this problem, rather than the general effects of policy on prices or the value of money, that necessarily preoccupies the central banker in his day-to-day actions. It is a task which makes it necessary for the central bank constantly to forestall or counteract developments in the realm of credit, for which no simple rules can provide sufficient guidance.[37]

The same is nearly as true of the measures intended to affect prices and employment. They must be directed more at forestalling changes before they occur than at correcting them after they have occurred. If a central bank always waited until rule or mechanism forced it to take action, the resulting fluctuations would be much greater than they need be. And if, within the range of its discretion, it takes measures in a direction opposite to those which mechanism or rule will later impose upon it, it will probably create a situation in which the mechanism will not long be allowed to operate. In the last resort, therefore, even where the discretion of the authority is greatly restricted, the outcome is likely to depend on what the authority does within the limits of its discretion.

---

[37] See my essay 'Monetary Nationalism and International Stability'.

This means in practice that under present conditions we have little choice but to limit monetary policy by prescribing its goals rather than its specific actions. The concrete issue today is whether it ought to keep stable some level of employment or some level of prices. Reasonably interpreted and with due allowance made for the inevitability of minor fluctuations around a given level, these two aims are not necessarily in conflict, provided that the requirements for monetary stability are given first place and the rest of economic policy is adapted to them. A conflict arises, however, if 'full employment' is made the chief objective and this is interpreted, as it sometimes is, as that maximum of employment which can be produced by monetary means in the short run. That way lies progressive inflation.

The reasonable goal of a high and stable level of employment can probably be secured as well as we know how while aiming at the stability of some comprehensive price level. For practical purposes, it probably does not greatly matter precisely how this price level is defined, except that it should not refer exclusively to final products (for if it did, it might in times of rapid technological advance still produce a significant inflationary tendency), and that it should be based as much as possible on international rather than local prices. Such a policy, if pursued simultaneously by two or three of the major countries, should also be reconcilable with stability of exchange rates. The important point is that there will be definite known limits which the monetary authorities will not allow price movements to exceed—or even to approach to the point of making drastic reversals of policy necessary.

Weak Opposition to Inflation
Though there may be some people who explicitly advocate continuous inflation, it is certainly not because the majority wants it that we are likely to get it. Few people would be willing to accept it when it is pointed out that even such a seemingly moderate increase in prices as 3 percent per annum means that the price level will double every twenty-three and a half years and that it will nearly quadruple over

the normal span of a man's working life. The danger that inflation will continue is not so much due to the strength of those who deliberately advocate it as to the weakness of the opposition. In order to prevent it, it is necessary for the public to become clearly aware of the things we can do and of the consequences of not doing them. Most competent students agree that the difficulty of preventing inflation is only political and not economic. Yet almost no one seems to believe that the monetary authorities have the power to prevent it and will exercise it. The greatest optimism about the short-term miracles that monetary policy will achieve is accompanied by a complete fatalism about what it will produce in the long run.

There are two points which cannot be stressed enough: first, it seems certain that we shall not stop the drift toward more and more state control unless we stop the inflationary trend; and, second, any continued rise in prices is dangerous because, once we begin to rely on its stimulating effect, we shall be committed to a course that will leave us no choice but that between more inflation, on the one hand, and paying for our mistake by a recession or depression, on the other. Even a very moderate degree of inflation is dangerous because it ties the hands of those responsible for policy by creating a situation in which, every time a problem arises, a little more inflation seems the only easy way out.

We have not had space to touch on the various ways in which the efforts of individuals to protect themselves against inflation, such as sliding-scale contracts, not only tend to make the process self-accelerating but also increase the rate of inflation necessary to maintain its stimulating effect. Let us simply note, then, that inflation makes it more and more impossible for people of moderate means to provide for their old age themselves; that it discourages saving and encourages running into debt; and that, by destroying the middle class, it creates that dangerous gap between the completely propertyless and the wealthy that is so characteristic of societies which have gone through prolonged inflations and which is the source of so much tension in those societies. Perhaps even more ominous is the wider psychological effect, the spreading among the population at large of that disregard of long-range views and exclusive concern with immediate advantages which already dominate public policy.

It is no accident that inflationary policies are generally advocated by those who want more government control—though, unfortunately, not by them alone. The increased dependence of the individual upon government which inflation produces and the demand for more government action to which this leads may for the socialist be an argument in its favour. Those who wish to preserve freedom should recognise, however, that inflation is probably the most important single factor in that vicious circle wherein one kind of government action makes more and more government control necessary. For this reason all those who wish to stop the drift toward increasing government control should concentrate their efforts on monetary policy. There is perhaps nothing more disheartening than the fact that there are still so many intelligent and informed people who in most other respects will defend freedom and yet are induced by the immediate benefits of an expansionist policy to support what, in the long run, must destroy the foundations of a free society.

(*The Constitution of Liberty,* pp. 330–33, 336–39)

VI. Main Themes Restated

18. Personal Recollections of Keynes

Professor Hayek here brings together some of the major threads in his criticisms of Keynes and the macro approach. He points out that the Keynesian concept of what may be called 'full' unemployment assumes implicitly that all resources are freely available and that consequently any increase in money incomes will increase output, thus reviving the inflationist fallacies which in 1931 he had supposed to have been eradicated. Professor Hayek emphasises that the Keynesian mode of thinking systematically eliminates from consideration those price inter-relationships which operate in the real world; that the General Theory *was, in very large part, simply a tract for the times.*

Even to those who knew Keynes but could never bring themselves to accept his monetary theories, and at times thought his pronouncements somewhat irresponsible, the personal impression of the man remains unforgettable. And especially to my generation (he was my senior by sixteen years) he was a hero long before he achieved real fame as an economic theorist. Was he not the man who had had the courage to protest against the economic clauses of the peace treaties of 1919? We admired the brilliantly written books for their outspokenness and independence of thought, even though some older and acuter thinkers at once pointed out certain theoretical flaws in his argument. And those of us who had the good fortune to meet him personally soon experienced the magnetism of the brilliant conversationalist with his wide range of interests and his bewitching voice.

I met him first in 1928 in London at some meeting of institutes of business cycle research, and though we had at once our first strong disagreement on some point of interest theory, we remained thereafter friends who had many interests in common, although we rarely could agree on economics. He had a somewhat intimidating manner in which he would try to ride roughshod over the objections of a younger man, but if one stood up to him he would respect him forever afterwards even if he disagreed. After I moved from Vienna to London in 1931 we had much occasion for discussion both orally and by correspondence.

Keynes Changes His Mind

I had undertaken to review for *Economica* his *Treatise on Money* which had then just appeared, and I put a great deal of work into two long articles on it. To the first of these he replied by a counterattack on my *Prices and Production*. I felt that I had largely demolished his theoretical scheme (essentially Vol. I), though I had great admiration for the many profound but unsystematical insights contained in Volume II of the work. Great was my disappointment when all this effort seemed wasted because after the appearance of the second part of my article he told me that he had in the meantime changed his mind and no longer believed what he had said in that work.

This was one of the reasons why I did not return to the attack when he published his now famous *General Theory*—a fact for which I later much blamed myself. But I feared that before I had completed my analysis he would again have changed his mind. Though he had called it a 'general' theory, it was to me too obviously another tract for the times, conditioned by what he thought were the momentary needs of policy. But there was also another reason which I then only dimly felt but which in retrospect appears to me the decisive one: my disagreement with that book did not refer so much to any detail of the analysis as to the general approach followed in the whole work. The real issue was the validity of what we now call macro-analysis, and I feel now that in a long-run perspective the chief significance of the *General Theory* will appear that more than any other single work it decisively furthered the ascendancy of macro-economics and the temporary decline of micro-economic theory.

I shall later explain why I think that this development is fundamentally mistaken. But first I want to say that it is rather an irony of fate that Keynes should have become responsible for this swing to macro-theory. Because he thought in fact rather little of the kind of econometrics which was just then becoming popular, and I do not think that he owed any stimulus to it. His ideas were rooted entirely in Marshallian economics, which was in fact the only economics he knew. Widely read as Keynes was in many fields, his education in economics was somewhat narrow. He did not read any foreign language except French—or, as he once said of himself, in German he could understand only what he knew already. It is a curious fact that before World War I he had reviewed Ludwig von Mises's *Theory of Money* for the *Economic Journal* (just as A.C. Pigou had a little earlier reviewed Wicksell) without in any way profiting from it. I fear it must be admitted that before he started to develop his own theories, Keynes was not a highly trained or a very sophisticated economic theorist. He started from a rather elementary Marshallian economics and what had been achieved by Walras and Pareto, the Austrians and the Swedes was very much a closed book to him. I have reason to doubt whether he ever fully mastered the theory of international trade; I don't think he had ever thought systematically on the theory of capital, and even in the theory of the value of money his starting point—and later the object of his criticism—appears to have been a very simple, equation-of-exchange-type of the quantity theory rather than the much more sophisticated cash-balances approach of Alfred Marshall.

Thinking in Aggregates

He certainly from the beginning was much given to thinking in aggregates and always had *faible* for the (sometimes very tenuous) global estimates. Already in discussion of the 1920s arising out of Great Britain's return to the Gold Standard his argument had been couched entirely in terms of price- and wage-levels in practically complete disregard of the structure of relative prices and wages, and later the belief that, because they were statistically measurable, such averages and the various aggregates were also causally of central importance, appears to have gained increasing hold upon him. His final conceptions rest entirely on the belief that there exist relatively simple and constant functional relationships between such 'measurable' aggregates as total demand, investment, or output, and that empirically established values of these presumed 'constants' would enable us to make valid predictions.

There seems to me, however, not only to exist no reason whatever to assume that these 'functions' will remain constant, but I believe that micro-theory had demonstrated long before Keynes that they cannot be constant but will change over time not only in quantity but even in sign. What these relationships will be, which all macro-economics must treat as quasi-constant, depends indeed on the micro-economic structure, especially on the relations between different prices which macro-economics systematically disregards. They may change very rapidly as a result of changes in the micro-economic structure, and conclusions based on the assumption that they are constant are bound to be very misleading.

Let me use as an illustration the relation between the demand for consumers' goods and the volume of investment. There are undoubtedly certain conditions in which an increase of the demand for consumers' goods *will* lead to an increase of investment. But Keynes assumes that this will always be the case. It can easily be demonstrated, however, that this cannot be so and that in some circumstances an increase of the demand for final products must lead to a *decrease* of investment.

The first will generally be true only if, as Keynes generally assumes, there exist unemployed reserves of all factors of production and of the various kinds of commodities. In such circumstances it is possible at the same time to increase the production of consumers' goods and the production of capital goods.

The position is altogether different, however, if the economic system is in a state of full or nearly full employment. Then it is possible to increase the output of investment goods only by at least temporarily reducing the output of consumers' goods, because to increase the production of the former, factors will have to be shifted to it from the production of consumers' goods. And it will be some time before the additional investment helps to increase the flow of consumers' goods.

Full Employment Assumption

Keynes appears to have been misled here by a mistake opposite to that of which he accused the classical economists. He alleged, with only partial justification, that the classics had based their argument on the assumption of full employment, and he based his own argument on what may be called the assumption of full *un*employment, i.e., the assumption that there normally existed unused reserves of *all* factors and commodities. But the latter assumption is not only at least as unlikely to be true in fact as the former; it is also much more misleading. An analysis on the assumption of full employment, even if the assumption is only partially valid, at least helps us to understand the functioning of the price mechanism, the significance of the relations between different prices and of the factors which lead to a change in these relations. But the assumption that all goods and factors are available in excess makes the whole price system redundant, undetermined and unintelligible. Indeed some of the most orthodox disciples of Keynes appear consistently to have thrown overboard all the traditional theory of price determination and of distribution, all that used to be the backbone of economic theory, and in consequence, in my opinion, to have ceased to understand any economics.

It is easy to see how such belief, according to which the creation of additional money will lead to the creation of a corresponding amount of goods, was bound to lead to a revival of the more naïve inflationist fallacies which we thought economics had once and for all exterminated. And I have little doubt that we owe much of the post-war inflation to the great influence of such over-simplified Keynesianism. Not that Keynes himself would have approved of this. Indeed, I am fairly certain that if he had lived he would in that period have been one of the most determined fighters against inflation. About the last time I saw him, a few weeks before his death, he more or less plainly told me so. As his remark on that occasion is illuminating in other respects, it is worth reporting. I had asked him whether he was not getting alarmed about the use to which some of his disciples were putting his theories. His reply was that these theories had been greatly needed in the 1930s, but if these theories should ever become harmful, I could be assured that he would quickly bring about a change in public opinion. What I blame him for is that he had called such a tract for the times the *General Theory*.

The fact is that, although he liked to pose as the Cassandra whose dire predictions were not listened to, he was really supremely confident of his powers of persuasion and believed that he could play on public opinion as a virtuoso plays on his instrument. He was, by gift and temperament, more an artist and politician than a scholar or student. Though endowed with supreme mental powers, his thinking was as much influenced by aesthetic and intuitive as by purely rational factors. Knowledge came easy to him and he possessed a remarkable memory. But the intuition which made him sure of the results before he had demonstrated them, and led him to justify the same policies in turn by very different theoretical arguments, made him rather impatient of the slow, painstaking intellectual work by which knowledge is normally advanced.

He was so many-sided that for his estimate as a man it seemed almost irrelevant that one thought his economics to be both false and dangerous. If one considers how small a share of his time and energy he gave to economics, his influence on economics and the fact that he will be remembered chiefly as an economist is both miraculous and tragic. He would be remembered as a great man by all who knew him even if he had never written on economics.

I cannot from personal knowledge speak of his services to his country during the last five or six years of his life when, already a sick man, he gave all his energy to public service. Yet it was during those years when I saw most of him and came to know him fairly well. The London School of Economics had at the outbreak of war been moved to Cambridge, and when it became necessary in 1940 for me to live wholly at Cambridge, he found quarters for me at his College. On the weekends for which, so far as possible, he sought the quiet of Cambridge, I then saw a fair amount of him and came to know him otherwise than merely professionally. Perhaps it was because he was seeking relief from his arduous duties, or because all that concerned his official work was secret, that all his other interests then came out most clearly. Though he had before the war reduced his business connections and given up the bursarships of his college, the interests and activities he still actively pursued besides his official duties would have taxed the whole strength of most other men. He kept as informed on artistic, literary and scientific matters as in normal times, and always his strong personal likings and dislikings came through.

Wide Intellectual Interests
I remember particularly one occasion which now seems to me characteristic of many. The war was over and Keynes had just returned from an official mission to Washington on a matter of the greatest consequence which one would have assumed had absorbed all his energy. Yet he entertained a group of us for part of the evening with

details about the state of the collection of Elizabethan books in the United States as if the study of this had been the sole purpose of his visit. He was himself a distinguished collector in this field, as of manuscripts of about the same period, and of modern paintings.

As I mentioned before, his intellectual interests were also largely determined by aesthetic predilections. This applied as much to literature and history as to other fields. Both the 16th and 17th centuries greatly appealed to him, and his knowledge, at least in selected parts, was that of an expert. But he much disliked the 19th century and would occasionally show a lack of knowledge of its economic history and even the history of its economics surprising in an economist.

I cannot in this short essay attempt even to sketch the general philosophy and outline on life which guided Keynes's thinking. It is a task which has yet to be attempted, because on this the otherwise brilliant and remarkably frank biography by Sir Roy Harrod is hardly sufficient—perhaps because he so completely shared and therefore took for granted the peculiar brand of rationalism which dominated Keynes's generation. Those who want to learn more about this I would strongly advise to read Keynes's own essay 'My Early Beliefs' which was published in a little volume entitled *Two Memoirs*.

In conclusion I want to say a few words about the future of Keynesian theory. Perhaps it will be evident from what I have already said that I believe that this will be decided not by any future discussion of his special theorems but rather by the future development of views on the appropriate method of the social sciences. Keynes's theories will appear merely as the most prominent and influential instance of a general approach whose philosophical justification seems to be highly questionable. Though with its reliance on apparently measurable magnitudes it *appears* at first more scientific than the older microtheory, it seems to me that it has achieved this pseudo-exactness at the price of disregarding the relationships which really govern the economic system. Even though the schemata of micro-economics do not claim to achieve those quantitative predictions at which the ambitions of macro-economics aim, I believe by learning to content ourselves with the more modest aims of the former, we shall gain more insight into at least the principle on which the complex order of economic life operates, than by the artificial simplification necessary for macro-theory which tends to conceal nearly all that really matters. I venture to predict that once this problem of method is settled, the 'Keynesian Revolution' will appear as an episode during which erroneous conceptions of the appropriate scientific method led to the temporary obliteration of many important insights which we had already achieved and which we shall then have painfully to regain.

(Personal Recollections of Keynes & the 'Keynesian Revolution')

19. GENERAL AND RELATIVE WAGES

Two major points are made in these two extracts (from a draft of an essay on Competition As A Discovery Procedure—*published later in a revised form in German).*

Professor Hayek first emphasises the role of the pricing system, and especially of price changes, as a means of adapting the economy to the unforeseeable changes that make up the real world. Without such continuous adaptations real income and the stock of real resources would necessarily be lower than they could *be with an optimal use of the pricing system. Professor Hayek here develops the concept of the pricing system as a transmitter of empirical knowledge, a concept first systematically propounded in his early essays on 'Economics and Knowledge' (1937), and 'The Use of Knowledge in Society' (1945).*

Applying this approach to the labour sector, Professor Hayek, in the second extract, shows the role of changes in relative wage rates in reallocating labour between industries, thus facilitating the continuous adaptation to ever-changing circumstances necessary even for the maintenance of real income and wealth. Where such changes in wage rates are prevented by institutions, such as unions, the aggregate real income of the community is kept below the level it might have reached.

The inefficacy of non-market wage-rate fixing, whether by trade unions or other bodies, as a method of raising the real incomes of all *members of the working class is argued here.*

The consequences of this misinterpretation of the market as an economy that can and ought to satisfy different needs in a predetermined order of importance, are particularly evident in the efforts of policy to alter prices and incomes in the interest of what is called 'social justice'. Whatever meaning social philosophers have attached to this concept, in the practice of economic policy it has almost exclusively meant only one thing: the protection of groups against the necessity of a descent from the absolute or relative material positions that they have for some time occupied in society. Yet this is not a principle on which it is possible to act generally without destroying the whole foundation of the market order. Not only the continuous increase but in some circumstances even the maintenance of the present level of real income depends on adapting to unforeseen changes; such adaptation involves a reduction in the relative and perhaps even the absolute share of some, although they are in no way responsible for the situation.

Unpredictability and the Price System
The point which we must constantly keep in mind is that *all* economic adjustment is made necessary by unforeseen changes; the whole point of employing the price mechanism is to inform individuals that what they have been doing or can do is now in greater or lesser demand for some reason which is no responsibility of theirs. Adaptation of the whole order of activities to changed circumstances rests on changes in the remuneration offered for different activities, without regard to the deserts or faults of those concerned.

The term 'incentives' is often used in this connection, with the somewhat misleading connotation that the main problem is to induce people to exert themselves sufficiently. The main guidance which prices offer us is however not *how much* but *what* to do. In a continuously changing world even maintaining a given level of wealth requires continuous changes in the activities of some, that will be brought about only if the remuneration of some activities is increased and that of others decreased. These adjustments are needed merely to maintain the total income stream under relatively stable conditions; no 'surplus' will be achieved under them, which could be used to compensate those injured by changing prices. Only in a rapidly growing catallaxy can we hope to avoid absolute declines in the position of some.

Modern economists often seem to overlook that even the relative stability shown by many of those aggregates which macro-economics treats as data is itself the result of a micro-economic process of which changes in relative prices are an essential part. It is only thanks to the market mechanism that another is induced to step in and fill the gap caused by the failure of one to fulfill the expectations of his partners. In fact all those aggregate demand and supply curves with which we like to operate are not really objective given facts but results of the continuous processes of the market. Nor can we hope to learn from statistical information what alterations in prices or incomes are necessary to bring about adjustments to such inevitable changes. But the chief point is that in a democratic society it would be wholly impossible to bring changes about by commands which are not felt to be just and whose necessity can never be clearly demonstrated. Deliberate regulation in such a political system must always aim to secure prices which appear just, which in practice means preserving the traditional income and price structure. But an economic system in which each gets what the others think he 'deserves' would necessarily be highly inefficient—quite apart from also being an intolerably oppressive system. Every 'incomes policy' is therefore likely to prevent rather than facilitate those changes in the price and income structure that are required to adapt the system to changed conditions.

It is one of the paradoxes of the present world that the communist countries are probably freer than the 'capitalist' countries from the incubus of 'social justice' and more willing to let those suffer against whom developments turn. At least for some Western countries the position is so hopeless precisely because the ideology which at present dominates politics makes those changes well-nigh impossible that would be necessary in order to bring about that rapid further rise in the position of the working class which, in turn, would eclipse this ideology.

Wage Rigidities

Market forces are relatively sturdy; they tend to reassert themselves in the most unexpected manner when we think we have driven them out. Nonetheless in the Western world we have succeeded in isolating the most ubiquitous factor of production from such forces. It is generally accepted that the most severe difficulties of contemporary economic policy are due to what is usually described as the rigidity of wages, which means in effect that both the wage structure and the level of money wages have increasingly become impervious to market forces. This rigidity is usually treated by economists as irreversible, so that we must adapt our policies to it. For thirty years the discussion of monetary policy has been concerned almost entirely with the search for expedients by which to circumvent it. I have long felt that these monetary devices provide merely a *temporary* way out, and can but postpone the day when we will have to face the central issue. They also make the real solution, which cannot forever be avoided, more difficult because by accepting these rigidities as unalterable we increase them and give the sanction of legitimacy to what are anti-social and destructive practices. I have largely lost interest in current discussions on monetary policy because it seems to me that in its failure to face up to the central issue, it passes the buck, in an irresponsible manner, on to our successors. We are of course in this respect already reaping the harvest of the work of the man who set this fashion since we are already in that long run in which he knew we would be dead.

It is a great misfortune for the world that these theories were formed as a result of an exceptional and unique situation in which it could be properly argued that the problem of unemployment was largely a problem of a too-high *level* of real wages, and in which the much more crucial and general problem of the flexibility of the wage *structure* could be neglected. As a result of Britain's return to gold in 1925 at the 1914 parity, a situation had been created in which it could be plausibly argued that *all* real wages in Britain had become too high for her to achieve the necessary volume of exports. I doubt whether the same has ever been true of any other important country, and even whether it was entirely true of the Britain of the 1920s. But of course Britain had then the oldest, most firmly entrenched and most comprehensive trade union movement in the world which by its wage policy had largely succeeded in establishing a wage structure determined much more by considerations of 'justice', which meant little else than the preservation of traditional wage differentials, and which made those changes in relative wages demanded by an adaptation to changed conditions 'politically impossible'. No doubt the situation then meant that full employment required that some real wages, perhaps those of many groups of workers, would have to be reduced from the position to which they had been raised by deflation. But nobody can say whether this would necessarily have meant a fall in the general level of *all* real wages. The adjustment of the structure of industry to the new condition that adjustments in wages would have induced might have made this unnecessary. But, unfortunately, the *fashionable* macro-economic emphasis on the *average* level of wages prevented this possibility from being seriously considered at the time.

Importance of Relative Wages

Let me put these conditions in a more general form. There can be little doubt that the productivity of labour, and hence the level of real wages, depends on its *distribution between* industries and occupations, and that the latter, in turn, depends on the structure of *relative* wages. If this wage structure has become more or less rigid, it will prevent or delay adjustments in industrial structure to changing conditions. It would seem probable that in a country in which the relations between different wage rates have long remained practically unchanged, the level of real wages at which full employment can be maintained would be considerably lower than it *could* be.

Indeed it would seem that without the rapid advance of technology and the relatively high level of capital formation to which we have become accustomed, a fully rigid wage structure would prevent most adaptations to changes in other conditions, including those necessary to maintain the initial level of incomes; wage-rate rigidities would thus lead to a gradual fall in the level of real wages at which full employment could be maintained. I know of no empirical studies of the relations between wage flexibility and growth but I should be inclined to expect that such a study would show a high positive correlation between the two magnitudes: not merely because growth will lead to changes in relative wages but even more because such *changes are essential* to adapt to the new conditions which growth requires.

But to return to what appears to me to be the crucial point: I have suggested that the level of real wages at which full employment can be maintained is dependent on the structure of relative wages, and that in consequence, if this structure is rigid and the relation between wages remains constant while conditions change, the level of real wages at which full employment can be maintained will tend to fall, or at least not rise as fast as it might because of the beneficial effects of other circumstances. This would mean that the manipulation of the level of real wages by monetary policy is not really a way out of the difficulties which the rigidity of the wage structure creates. Nor can we expect that any sort of 'incomes policy' or the like will offer a way out. In the end it will prove that the very rigidity in the wage structure which trade unions have created in the presumed interest of their members is one of the greatest obstacles to the advance of the real income of the working classes as a whole: real wages and other incomes will not rise as fast as they could if some real wages were allowed to fall, absolutely or at least relatively.

The classical aim, which, in the words of John Stuart Mill, was 'full employment at high wages', can therefore be achieved only by an efficient use of labour which requires the *free* movement of *relative* wage rates. That illustrious man, whose name for this reason I believe will go down to history as the grave digger of the British economy, chose instead full employment at low wages. For this is the necessary result if the rigidity of relative wages is accepted as unalterable, and attempts made to correct its effects by lowering the general level of real wages by the roundabout process of lowering the value of money. We see now clearly that this evasion of the central issue has offered only a temporary way out and that we have probably reached the point when we must face the evil at its source. We can no longer close our eyes to the fact that the interests of the working class as a whole demand that the power of particular labour unions to preserve the status of their members be *curbed*. The practical problem seems now to be how we may assure the working class as a whole that if the status of particular groups is not protected, this policy will not only not endanger but indeed enhance the prospects of a rise in its real wages.

(*From a draft paper referred to in the introductory note*)

20. CARACAS CONFERENCE REMARKS

In this final extract Professor Hayek graphically illustrates the dilemma created by inflation, which leaves the economy, as he says, grasping a 'tiger by the tail'. Unless there is a continuous acceleration in the rate *of increase of prices, recessionary symptoms begin to appear . . . so that ultimately the choice is between a runaway inflation and an extensive depression and readjustment to a non-inflationary situation.*

Twenty years ago I lost interest in monetary matters because of my disillusionment with Bretton Woods. I was wrong in my prediction that the arrangement would soon disappear. Its main innovation has been to impose the responsibility for restoring balance in international payments on the creditor nations. This was reasonable in the deflationary 1930s, but not in an inflationary period. Now we have an inflation-borne prosperity which depends for its continuation on continued inflation. If prices rise less than expected, then a depressing effect is exerted on the economy. I expected that ten years would suffice to produce increasing difficulty; however, it has taken 25 years to reach the stage where to slow down inflation produces a recession. We now have a tiger by the tail: how long can this inflation continue? If the tiger (of inflation) is freed he will eat us up; yet if he runs faster and faster while we desperately hold on, we are *still* finished! I'm glad I won't be here to see the final outcome . . .

>(Notes of comments by F.A. Hayek on a paper presented to the Mont Pèlerin Conference, Caracas)

VII. The Outlook for the 1970s: Open or Repressed Inflation?

By F.A. Hayek

In the last 40 years monetary policy has increasingly committed us to a development which has recurrently made necessary further measures that weakened the functioning of the market mechanism. We have now reached a point when it is widely proposed to combat the effects of our policy by further controls which would not only make the price mechanism wholly ineffective, but also make inevitable an ever-increasing central direction of all economic activity.

The development began with the acceptance of the given structure of money wages as not capable of being altered by the lowering of any wages, and the consequent demand that total money expenditure be raised sufficiently to take up the whole supply of labour at whatever wage rates prevailed. The result of this policy has been not only greatly to increase resistance to the lowering *of any* wage, but also to remove the main safeguard in the past to pushing wages above the point where the current supply of labour could be sold without further monetary expansion; i.e., to remove the acknowledged responsibility of the trade unions for the unemployment caused by their wage policies.

Long-run Vicious Circle
That it is always possible temporarily to reduce unemployment by a sufficient degree of monetary expansion was of course never doubted

by anyone who had studied the major inflations of the past. If nevertheless the deliberate use of inflation to reduce unemployment was opposed by some economists, it was because of their belief that the employment thus created could be maintained only by continued and probably even progressive inflation. The reliance on what appears in the short-run as the politically easy way out thus tends to preserve and intensify a disequilibrium position in which the maintenance of an adequate volume of employment would require ever more drastic doses of inflation.

These apprehensions have been fully confirmed by the developments since the war. A continuing moderate degree of monetary expansion has proved insufficient to secure lasting full employment. There are two important reasons for this failure. Inflation tends not only to preserve but to increase the maldistribution of labour between industries, which must produce unemployment as soon as inflation ceases. Secondly, some of the stimulating effects of inflation are due to prices being for a time higher than expected, so that many undertakings are successful which would have failed if prices had not risen.

But a given rate of price increases comes to be expected after it has continued for some time, and the stimulating effect of inflation will therefore be maintained only if the rate of increase of prices accelerates and runs ahead of the expected rate of increase of prices. A continuing constant rate of increase of prices, on the other hand, must soon create a position in which future prices are correctly anticipated and present costs adapted to these expectations, with the result that the gains due to inflation disappear.

The magnitude of unemployment caused by a cessation of inflation will increase with the length of the period during which such policies are pursued. It not only becomes politically more and more difficult for policy to extricate itself from the train of events it has set up, but governments facing reelection find themselves recurrently forced to speed up inflation to whatever degree proves necessary to secure an acceptable level of employment.

While a mild degree of inflation is widely regarded as not too high a price for securing a high level of employment, the fact that inflation achieves this result only if it accelerates means that sooner or later the other effects of inflation will cause increasing discontent and a growing dislocation of economic processes. There are many harmful effects of inflation through which it endangers the efficiency, stability and growth of production, but that which first tends to cause widespread discontent is the effect of rising prices for consumers' goods on those classes whose incomes, for one reason or another, do not keep pace with the rise of prices. It is the complaints of groups who find themselves poorer as a result of the increased costs of living that usually impel the first steps to combat inflation. These consist of attempts to prohibit or otherwise prevent the rise of prices caused by demand overtaking supply.

All measures of this kind do not of course remove the cause of the rise of prices but serve rather to make it possible for governments to continue with their inflationary policies without the effects manifesting themselves in the way in which they are most rapidly noticed. Because in a free market the general rise of prices is the most conspicuous sign of an excess of the stream of money expenditure over the stream of goods and services to be bought, people tend to think that if prices stop rising the evil of inflation has been conquered.

Repressed Inflation a Special Evil

It is probably no exaggeration to say that, although open inflation that manifests itself in a rise of prices is a great evil, it is less harmful than a repressed inflation—i.e., an increase of money which does not lead to a rise of prices because price increases are effectively prohibited. Such repressed inflation makes the price mechanism wholly inoperative and leads to its progressive replacement by central direction of all economic activity.

It is very doubtful, moreover, whether, after the imposition of price ceilings, the excess supply of money will still secure full employment.

A significant part of the existing employment will have been based on the expectation of a further rise of prices which will now be disappointed. And in so far as the increase in the supply of money is reduced, those goods and services on which the additional money first impinged will suffer a reduction of demand. It is, however, unlikely that in such a situation the increase of the amount of money will stop. Since its immediate effects are rendered less obvious, it is likely to continue and to build up a further 'overhang' of excess money (i.e., cash holdings people would wish to spend if the commodities they wanted were available) which will make a removal of the imposed controls more and more difficult.

Preventing the rise of prices does not of course secure that everyone can buy more than they would if prices had risen. Instead of being certain to be able to buy goods and services at known though rising prices with the money they have to spend, buyers will be faced with shortages; who will get the available goods will be determined by accident or the favour of the sellers, and sooner or later inevitably by a more formal system of rationing.

The allocation of resources will at first still be determined by the structure of prices frozen after being distorted by inflation. These frozen relative prices will of course no longer be able to bring about the adjustment of production to changing conditions and needs. Consequently the direction of production will also have to be increasingly determined by decisions of government.

Central Control and 'Politically Impossible' Changes
This process by which attempts to control inflation by price ceilings lead to ever more comprehensive governmental controls, is self-accelerating also, because once production becomes dependent on rationing, licensing, permissions and official allocations, a constant overhang of money becomes necessary to keep goods flowing. No centrally directed economy has yet been able to operate without

relying on the effect of an excess supply of money to help overcome the obstacles it creates.

The ultimate transition to a centrally directed economy seems thus inevitable if inflation is allowed to continue while its effects are partly suppressed by a price stop. There seems little prospect that governments in such a situation will effectively prevent further inflation and not merely suppress its most visible consequences. As inflation becomes more rapid the demand for its discontinuance will also become more pressing, but the amount of unemployment caused by every slowing down of inflation will simultaneously increase. We can probably expect governments to make repeated further attempts to slow down inflation, only to abandon them when the unemployment they produce becomes politically unacceptable.

It is to be feared that we have already reached a stage in this process when to save the market economy will call for much more drastic changes in our institutions than most commentators are ready to contemplate or than will be thought by many to be 'politically possible'.[1] There seems little immediate prospect that we shall be able directly to eliminate that determination of wages by collective bargaining which is the ultimate cause of the inflationary trend,[2] or that we can reimpose upon trade unions the restraint which in the past stemmed from the fear of causing extensive unemployment. The only hope of escape from the vicious circle would seem to be to persuade the trade unions that it is in the interest of the workers in general to agree to an alternative method of wage determination which, while offering the workers as a whole a better chance of material advance, at the same time restores the flexibility of the relative wages of particular groups.

---

[1] See W.H. Hutt, *Politically Impossible...?*, Hobart Paperback 1 (London: IEA, 1971).

[2] Professor James E. Meade has proposed limits on trade union wage-bargaining power in *Wages and Prices in a Mixed Economy,* Wincott Memorial Lecture, published as Occasional Paper 35 (London: IEA, 1971).

Profit-sharing a Solution
The only solution of this problem I can conceive is that the workers be persuaded to accept part of their remuneration, not in the form of a fixed wage, but as a participation in the profits of the enterprise by which they are employed. Suppose that, instead of a fixed total, they could be induced to accept an assured sum equal to, say, 80 percent of their past wages *plus* a share in profits which in otherwise unchanged conditions would give them on the average their former real income, but, in addition, a share in the growth of output of growing industries. In such a case the market mechanism would again be made to operate and at the same time one of the main obstacles to the growth of the social product would be removed.

This is not the place to develop in detail a suggestion which evidently raises many difficult problems. It is only mentioned to indicate that if we want to stop the process of cumulative inflation we shall have to consider much more radical changes in existing institutions than have yet been contemplated. If the dangers of present trends are clearly recognised, it may not be too late to extricate ourselves from a development in which we increasingly lose power over our fate. But unless we soon remedy the basic cause, we may find ourselves irrevocably committed to a path which leads to the destruction of far more than the material basis of our civilisation: not only economic progress but political and intellectual freedom would be threatened.

Basic Causes of Inflation
What is clear is that we must completely change the direction in which we have been endeavouring to reform the international monetary system during the last 25 years. Ever since Bretton Woods and the concern with the supposed lack of 'international liquidity', all efforts culminating in the creation of Special Drawing Rights have been aimed at enabling individual countries to inflate sufficiently to produce the maximum of employment which can be secured in the short run by monetary pressure. Now when it is becoming evident

that employment is not simply a function of total demand, and that a rise in total money expenditure may indeed increase the part of employment dependent on a further rise in expenditure, it is crucially important that we turn our attention to the more fundamental factors governing employment: namely, the adjustment of the labour force and the structure of relative wages to the continuous changes in the direction of demand.

It should always have been obvious that whether a given total of money expenditure is sufficient to take off the market the amount of labour offered will depend on how this money expenditure is distributed between the different commodities and services relative to the distribution of labour devoted to their production. However much money may be spent on some part of total output, it will not secure the employment of those who produce more of other commodities than is demanded, certainly in the short run and not even in the long run.

The illusion that maladjustments in the allocation of resources and of *relative* prices can be cured by a manipulation of the *total* quantity of money is at the root of most of our difficulties. Such a use of monetary policy is more likely to aggravate than to reduce these maladjustments. Monetary policy can at most temporarily, but never in the long run, relieve us of the necessity to make changes in the use of resources required by changes in the real factors. It ought to aim at assisting this adjustment, not delaying it.

The fact that in the long run a market economy cannot operate effectively if relative wages are not determined by market forces has for a time been concealed by the effects of inflation. The time when this truth can be concealed by moderate inflation is probably past. And there clearly is a limit to the degree of inflation with which a market economy can operate. Combating inflation by price fixing makes the market inoperative even sooner.

If we want to preserve the market economy our aim must be to restore the effectiveness of the price mechanism. The chief obstacle to its functioning is trade union monopoly. It does not come from the side of money, and an exaggerated expectation of what can be achieved by monetary policy has diverted our attention from the chief causes. Though money may be one of them if it is mismanaged, monetary policy can do no more than prevent disturbances by *monetary* causes: it cannot remove those which come from other sources.

VIII. Addendum 1978

Introduction

By Sudha Shenoy

Professor Hayek's writings on inflation and monetary policy, during the six years since the publication of the first edition of this book, are contained in his other IEA publications: *Full Employment at Any Price?* (1975), *Choice in Currency* (1976) and *Denationalisation of Money* (1976 and 1978). This second edition has been enlarged by the addition of three early analyses of the Keynesian approach. These early articles are notable for Professor Hayek's anticipation of the kinds of difficulties now being encountered, after some thirty-odd years of attempting to maintain full employment by increasing the level of spending.

At this juncture, I should like to add a few condensed reflections on the distinction between the average price-index approach to the analysis of the effects of inflation, and the 'relative' price structure approach on which the following extracts are based. This distinction derives from the difference between two alternative views of prices. One view sees them as components in some general equilibrium system. The other sees prices as empirical reflectors of specific circumstances. Such a distinction would appear to be important for the continuing debate on the nature of inflation.

Virtually all analyses of inflation are couched in terms of a movement in an index of prices. 'Keynesian' and 'Chicago-ite' may differ over whether or not the money supply is active or merely adjusts passively; but neither school goes beyond the impact (if any) on (or *via*) a price index.

The 'Austrian' would agree with the Chicago-ite on the 'active' role of the money supply. But he departs fundamentally thereafter. He emphasises that changes in a price index *cannot* encompass the major dislocating effect of increases in the supply of money. A price index is a statistical construct—it is an *ex post facto* compilation from *previous* changes in individual prices. An increase in the money supply does *not* affect all prices simultaneously and equi-proportionately—it affects some first and other prices afterwards; it affects different prices differently and at different times.

Economic decision-makers (individuals, firms, families) face not a price 'index' but specific *individual* prices. Different economic units face different prices. In an inflationary context, their problem is *not* to forecast the change in a price index as calculated in the future; it is rather to judge the specific changes made by a changing money supply at a specific time on the specific prices they deal with, as opposed to all the other influences also acting on these prices. The 'average' such change, as calculated some time *later,* is basically irrelevant—it provides no guide to the *individual* price changes that *precede* the calculation of the change in the price-index. The knowledge that the money supply is increasing gives little help (if any) in *separating out* from all other components that component of individual price changes resulting from such an increase in the money supply.

Guiding Role of Individual Price Changes
It is individual price changes and price relationships that in practice guide production and employment. The *pattern* of output and employment is thus altered in accordance with a monetary change—the different lines of production and employment follow the same path as those particular price changes brought about by the change in the money supply. But these price changes now reflect increases in the

supply of money. They do not tell us whether or not the underlying *real* influences have changed in the same direction. The alterations in the pattern of output and employment made in response to these price changes are thus *dis*coordinated: the real changes brought about by the expansion cannot 'mesh' with changes that reflect *real* influences. As this lack of coordination becomes clear, resources have to be withdrawn from the former lines of output and employment and transferred into those lines that *do* correspond with the underlying pattern of relative real scarcities and preferences. Such transfers are not costless: higher capital and operating losses and higher unemployment are the necessary concomitants. Continuing monetary expansion implies a continuing and continuous *discoordination*—i.e., resources are rendered less productive than they might be.[1]

In this context, to reason in terms of any sort of general equilibrium model can be seriously misleading: such models must presuppose an 'evenly-rotating economy', in Professor Mises's graphic terminology.[2] The 'Austrian' position is that, in a world of continuous change, relative real scarcities and preferences themselves have to be rediscovered continuously.[3] Monetary expansion brings about price changes that are uncoordinated: they do not reflect real scarcities and preferences. The resulting patterns of output and employment therefore cannot be sustained. A price index by its very mode of construction abstracts from these real *relative* changes in the process of pricing. 'Indexation' of money payments would add yet another random and uncoordinated influence to an already uncoordinated situation. It

---

[1]The above argument is highly condensed; a more extended statement is in G.P. O'Driscoll, Jr., and Sudha R. Shenoy, 'Inflation, Recession, Stagflation', in E.G. Dolan (ed.), *Foundations of Modern Austrian Economics* (Lawrence, Kansas: Sheed and Ward, 1976); cf. F.A. Hayek, *Prices and Production* (London: Routledge and Kegan Paul, 1935), pp. 28–30.

[2]Ludwig von Mises, *Human Action* (Chicago: Regnery, 1966), pp. 244–56.

[3]F.A. Hayek, 'Competition as a Discovery Procedure', in *New Studies in Philosophy, Politics, Economics and the History of Ideas* (London: Routledge and Kegan Paul, 1978).

would not assist in the fundamental task of bringing about a better correspondence between the patterns of prices, available real resources, and preferences.

Sudha R. Shenoy
University of Newcastle
New South Wales
January, 1978

21. GOOD AND BAD UNEMPLOYMENT POLICIES

In 1944 Professor Hayek emphasised that sustainable *employment depends on an appropriate* distribution *of labour among the different lines of production. This distribution must change as circumstances change.* Sustainable *employment thus depends on appropriate changes in* relative *real wage-rates. If established producers—both unions and capitalists—prevent such relative changes from becoming effective, there follows an unnecessary rise in unemployment. Sustainable employment now depends on successfully tackling these established labour and capital monopolies.*

One of the obstacles to a successful employment policy is, paradoxically enough, that it is so comparatively easy quickly to reduce unemployment, or even almost to extinguish it, for the time being. There is always ready at hand a way of rapidly bringing large numbers of people back to the kind of employment they are used to, at no greater immediate cost than the printing and spending of a few extra millions. In countries with a disturbed monetary history this has long been known, but it has not made the remedy much more popular. In England the recent discovery of this drug has produced a somewhat intoxicating effect; and the present tendency to place exclusive reliance on its use is not without danger.

Though monetary expansion can afford quick relief, it can produce a lasting cure only to a limited extent. Few people will deny that monetary policy can successfully counteract the deflationary spiral into which every minor decline of activity tends to degenerate. This does not mean, however, that it is desirable that we should normally strain the instrument of monetary expansion to create the maximum amount of employment which it can produce in the short run. The trouble with such a policy is that it would be almost certain to aggravate the more fundamental or structural causes of unemployment and leave us in the end in a position worse than that from which we started.

Maladjustments

The main cause of this kind of unemployment is undoubtedly the disproportion between the distribution of labour among the different industries and the rates at which the output of these industries could be continuously absorbed. At the end of this war we shall, of course, be faced with a particularly difficult problem of this character. In the past the best known disproportion of this kind and, because of its connection with periodical slumps the most important, was the chronic over-development of all the industries making equipment for use in further production.

It is more than likely that these industries, because of the intermittent way in which they operated, have always had a larger labour force than they could *continuously* employ. And while it is not difficult to create by means of monetary expansion in those industries another burst of feverish activity which will create temporarily conditions of 'full employment', and even draw still more people into those industries, we are thereby making more difficult the task of maintaining even employment. A monetary policy aiming at a stable long-run position would indeed deliberately have to stop expansion *before* 'full employment' in those industries had been reached, in order to avoid a new maldirection of resources.

Though this is the most important single instance of structural maladjustments responsible for unemployment, the recurrent depression constitutes only part of our problem. The hard core of persistent unemployment is an even greater menace and is due largely to maldistributions of a different kind which monetary policy can do even less to cure. We must here face the fact that the problem of unemployment is in the last resort a wage problem—a fact which used to be well understood but which a conspiracy of silence has recently relegated into oblivion.

Wages and Mobility
Demand shifts constantly to new articles and industries, and the more rapidly we advance the more frequent such changes become. Though the increased speed of change will necessarily swell the numbers temporarily out of work while looking for a new job, it need not cause an increase of lasting unemployment, or a reduction in the demand for labour as a whole. If movement into the advancing industries were free, they should readily absorb those laid off elsewhere. The new development which more and more prevents this, and which has become the most serious cause of protracted unemployment, is the tendency of those established in the progressing industries to exclude newcomers. If the increase in demand in those industries leads, not to an increase of employment and output, but merely to an increase of the wages and profits of those already established, there will indeed be no new demand for labour to offset the decrease. If every gain of an industry is treated as the preserve of a closed group, to be taken out almost entirely in higher wages and profits, every shift of demand must add to the lasting unemployment.

The very special and almost unique experience of this country in the years after the pound was artificially raised to its former gold value has produced a fallacious preoccupation with the general wage level. Where such an artificial increase of the national wage level is the cause of unemployment, monetary manipulation is indeed the simplest way to cure it. Such a situation, however, is altogether exceptional and not likely to occur, except in consequence of currency fluctuations.

In normal times employment depends much more on the relation between wages in the different industries—or, rather, on the degree of mobility which the wage structure allows. There is little that monetary policy can positively achieve in this connection. Indeed, if Lord Keynes is right in emphasising that workers attach more importance to the nominal figure of their money wages than to real wages, any attempt to meet the problems of wage rigidity by monetary expansion can only increase the immobility which is the real trouble: if money wages are maintained in declining industries the workers will become even more hesitant to leave them in order to break the protective walls sheltering the privileged groups in the advancing industries.

The struggle against unemployment is in the last resort the same as the struggle against monopoly. Need it be added that on this fundamental issue we are *not* moving in the right direction? Or that it would be a poor service to the community to pretend that there is an easy way out which makes it unnecessary to face the basic difficulties?

Dangers Ahead

It is easy to see how much more serious our problems must become if the present fashion should prevail and if it should become the accepted doctrine that it is the task of monetary policy to make good any harm done by monopolistic wage policies. Even apart from the effect on those responsible for wage policy, who are thus excused the responsibility for the effect of their action on employment, the one-sided emphasis on monetary policy may not only deprive our efforts of full results, but also produce effects as unlooked for as they are undesirable.

While it is true that an intelligent monetary policy is a *sine qua non* of the prevention of large-scale unemployment, it is equally certain that it is not enough. Short of universal compulsion we shall never lastingly conquer unemployment until we succeed in breaking the rigidities of our economic system which we have allowed the monopolies of capitalists and labour to create. To forget this and to trust solely to monetary policy is the more dangerous as it may succeed long enough to make it impossible to try anything else: the more we are induced to delay the more difficult adjustments, because for the time being we seem to be able to keep things going, the greater the sector of our economic system will grow which can be kept going only by the artificial stimulus of credit expansion and ever-increasing Government investment.

It is a path which would force us into progressively increasing Government control of all economic life, and eventually into the totalitarian state.

('Good and Bad Unemployment Policies')

22. Full Employment Illusions

In this 1946 article Professor Hayek argues that even a continued increase in the demand for consumers' goods would not necessarily lead to a parallel increase in the demand for producers' goods. Continued increases in spending would not thus be sufficient to maintain 'full employment'. This happens because, as the boom continues, the rise in the demand for consumers' goods is met by switching from the use of fixed to circulating capital. Consequently, the demand for fixed capital eventually declines, as the demand for consumers' goods continues to rise. In these circumstances, to maintain or increase expenditure would not *prevent a decline in the producers' goods industries.*

The analysis Professor Hayek set out in 1946 thus predicted the appearance of 'stagflation' some 30 years before it emerged so unexpectedly.

It is a favourite trick of radical reformers to appropriate for a pet theory of their own some good word describing an attractive state of affairs, and then to accuse everyone who is not prepared to swallow their proposals of callously disregarding the social good at which they aim. At the moment the most dangerous of these catchwords which seems to describe merely a desirable state of affairs, but in fact conceals a particular theory about the manner and extent to which it can be achieved, is, of course, 'full employment'. There is reason to believe that even many of those who originally gave currency to this phrase are becoming apprehensive about the way it is being used.

In the writings of the learned men who first systematically used the phrase, it did not mean what it was bound to come to mean in popular discussion: a guarantee to everyone of the kind of work and pay to which he thinks himself to be entitled. But this does not diminish the responsibility of those who in the first instance deliberately chose a popular catchword for a highly technical concept. It is more than likely that the belief they have created that full employment in the popular sense can be easily and painlessly achieved will prove the greatest obstacle to a rational policy which really would provide the maximum opportunity of employment which can be created in a free society.

Money Expenditure and Employment
It is an old story that in most situations an increase in total money expenditure will for a time produce an increase in employment. This has of old been the stock argument of all inflationists and soft-money people. And any person who has lived through one of the great inflations can have little doubt that up to a point it is true. There is, however, a further lesson to be drawn from the experience of these inflations which ought not to be forgotten. They have not only shown that a sufficient increase of final demand will usually increase employment; they have also shown that in order to maintain the level of employment thus achieved, credit expansion has to

go on at a certain progressive rate. This is shown particularly well by the great German inflation, during most of which the level of employment was very high. But as soon, and as often, as the rate was slowed down at which inflation progressed, unemployment at once reappeared, even though incomes and prices were still rising, yet at a somewhat slower rate than before.

An Old Argument in New Form
But if the substance of the argument is not new, the new hold it has gained on our generation is due to the fact that it has been restated in an original and apparently much improved form. If in the way in which it is usually propounded, this new theory is highly technical, the essence of it is very simple. What it amounts to is little more than the following: if all people were employed at the jobs they are seeking, total money income would be so and so much. Therefore, it is argued, if we increased total money income to the figure it would reach if everyone were employed, everybody will be employed. Could anything be simpler? All we need to do is to spend sufficient money so that aggregate expenditure can take care of the aggregate supply of labour at the wage figure for which men will hold out.

It is useful at once to test this theory on a situation which has occurred often in recent times. Assume that in any country there has been a great shift of demand from one group of industries to another. It does not matter whether the causes of this are changes in tastes, technological progress, or shifts in the channels of international trade. The first result will be, as was the case in so many countries in recent times, that we shall have a group of depressed industries side by side with others which are fairly prosperous. If then, as is the rule rather than the exception at present, labour in the progressive industries prefers to take out the gain in the form of higher wages rather than in larger employment, what will happen? Clearly the consequence will be that those who lose their jobs in the declining industries will have nowhere to go and remain unemployed.

There is much indication that a great part of modern unemployment is due to this cause. How much can the measures of so-called 'fiscal' policy or any inflationary measures accomplish against this kind of unemployment? The problem is clearly not merely one of the total volume of expenditure but of its distribution, and of the prices and wages at which goods and services are offered. Before leaving this simplified illustration, let me underline a few important facts which it brings out clearly and which are commonly overlooked.

The Shortcomings of Fiscal Policy

Firstly, it shows that the significant connection between wages and unemployment does not operate *via* changes in the general wage level. In the instance given it may well be that the general wage level will remain unchanged, and yet there can be no doubt that the unemployment is brought about by the rise of the wages of a certain group.

Secondly, this unemployment will not arise in the industries in which the wages are raised (which are the prosperous industries, in which the increase in wages merely prevents an expansion of employment and output), but in the depressed industries where wages will be either stationary or actually falling.

Thirdly, the illustration makes it easy to see how an attempt to cure this kind of unemployment by monetary expansion is bound to produce inflationary symptoms, and how the authority, if it persists in its attempt, will soon be forced to supplement its monetary policy by direct controls designed to conceal the symptoms of inflation. So long as the people insist on spending their extra income on the product of the industries where output is restricted by monopolistic policies of labour or capital, this will only tend to drive up wages and prices further but produce no significant effect on employment. If expansion is pressed further in the hope that ultimately enough of the extra income will spill over into the depressed industries, price control, rationing, or priorities will have to be applied to the prosperous industries. This is a very important point, and most of the expansionists make no bones about the fact that they mean to retain and even expand controls in order to prevent the extra money incomes which they propose to create, from going in 'undesirable' directions. There is little doubt that we shall see a good deal more of the same people on the one hand advocating more credit expansion, lower interest rates, etc., etc., and on the other demanding more controls in order to keep in check the inflation they are creating.

Cyclical Unemployment

The illustration I have given may seem to refer mainly to long-run or technological unemployment, and the advocates of the fashionable type of full employment policy will perhaps reply that they are mainly concerned with cyclical unemployment. This would, of course, be an admission that their 'full employment' is not really *full* employment in the sense in which the term is now popularly understood, but at most a cure of part of the unemployment we used to have in the past. The more careful defenders of the new policy often admit this. The late Lord Keynes, for instance, shortly before this war, once stated that England had reached practically full employment though the unemployment figure was still well over one million. This is not what the public has now been taught full employment to mean. And it will be inevitable in the present state of opinion that so long as such a strong remnant of unemployment remains there will be intense pressure for more of the same medicine, even though on the full employment theorists' own views it can do only harm and no good in such a situation.

It is more than doubtful, however, whether even so far as cyclical unemployment is concerned, the fashionable 'full employment' proposals offer more than a palliative, and whether in the long run their application may not make matters worse. To the extent that they merely aim at mitigating the deflationary forces in a depression, there has of course never been any question that in such a situation an easy money policy may help a recession from degenerating into a major slump. But the hopes and ambitions of the present 'full employment' school go much further. Its adherents believe that by merely maintaining money incomes at the level reached at the top of the boom they can permanently keep employment and production at the maximum figure reached. This is probably not only an illusion but a certain way to perpetuate the underlying causes of the decline in investment activity.

In many ways the problems of smoothing out cyclical fluctuations are similar to those created by shifts in demand between industries. The main difference is that in the case of the business cycle we have to deal not with what may be called horizontal shifts in demand, from industries producing one sort of final goods to those producing another, but with changes in the relative demand for consumers' goods and capital goods respectively. The decline in the demand for consumers' goods, which occurs in the later phases of the depression, is a consequence of the decline of employment and incomes in the industries producing capital goods: and the basic problem is why in the latter, employment and production periodically decline, long before any decrease in the demand for consumers' goods occurs.

The current belief, which inspires all the popular full employment propaganda, is of course that investment expenditure is directly dependent upon, and moves with consumers' expenditure and that therefore the more we spend the richer we get. This argument has a certain specious plausibility because in times of all around unemployment a mere revival of monetary demand may indeed lead to a proportional, or even more than proportional, increase in production. But it is utterly fallacious at other times and almost ridiculous if applied to the position which exists at the end of a boom and the onset of a depression. It is well worth while to examine its implications for a moment and to consider the paradox to which it leads if it is consistently followed.

Consumers' Goods Demand and Investment Activity
If it were true that an increase in the demand for consumers' goods always led to an increase of investment activity the consequences would indeed be astounding. It is important that at the top of the boom, or even at the early stages of an incipient depression, there are practically no unused resources available which would make it possible substantially to increase the output of investment goods without drawing labour and other resources away from the production of consumers' goods. In other words, if this curious theory were true it would mean that the result of people insistently demanding more consumers' goods would be that less consumers' goods would be produced for the time being. This in turn would undoubtedly lead to a rise in their prices and the profits made in their production, and according to the same theory this should lead to a still further stimulus to investment and therefore to another reduction in the current output of consumers' goods. This spiral would go on *ad infinitum,* presumably until a stage was reached when, because people so insistently demanded current consumers' goods, no consumers' goods at all would be currently produced and all energy devoted to create facilities for an increased future output of such goods.

Purchasing Power and Prosperity
The economic system is however not quite as crazy as all that. There indeed exists a mechanism through which in conditions of fairly full employment an increase of final demand, far from stimulating investment, will actually discourage it. This mechanism is very important both as an explanation of the break of the boom and for our understanding of the reasons why an attempt to maintain prosperity merely by maintaining purchasing power is bound to fail.

Why the Slump in Capital Goods Industries?
The mechanism in question operates in a way which will be familiar to most business men: Any given increase of prices will increase

percentage profits on working capital by more than profits on fixed capital. This is so because the same difference between prices and costs will be earned as many times more often as the capital is turned over more frequently during a given period of time. If, then, in a situation where prices of consumers' goods tend to rise, the capital at the disposal of a given firm is limited; the need for working capital, as experience amply demonstrates, regularly has precedence over the need for fixed capital. In other words, the limited capital resources of the individual firm will be spent in the way in which output can be most rapidly increased and the largest aggregate amount of profit earned on the given resources, i.e., in the form of working capital, and outlay on fixed capital will for the time being actually be reduced to make funds available for an increase of working capital.

There are many ways in which this can be done rapidly: working in double or treble shifts, neglect of repair and upkeep, or replacement by cheaper machinery, etc. If the inducement of high profits and the scarcity of funds is strong enough, this will sooner or later lead to an absolute reduction of the outlay on fixed capital.

So far this explains only why firms will allocate their capital outlay differently, more for working capital and less for fixed capital, and not why their total outlay falls, which is what we have to explain if we are to account for the slump in the capital goods industries. But we are in fact very close to an answer to this question and only one further step is needed.

The answer lies in a special application of a principle long known to economists under the name of 'the acceleration principle of derived demand'. It shows why the effect of any change in final demand on the volume of production in the 'earlier stages' of the processes in question will be multiplied in proportion to the amount of capital required. In the case of an increase of final demand the additional capacity will have to be created by installing machinery, building up stocks, etc., and for a time outlay will increase very much more than output. Similarly in the case of a decrease in final demand it will be possible for a time to decumulate stocks and machinery and outlay will be reduced more than output.

When we remember that this acceleration effect works both ways, positively and negatively, equally multiplying the effects of an increase or of a decrease of final demand many times insofar as the dependent investment demand is concerned, and that its strength depends on the amount of capital used per unit of output, it is easy to see what the results must be if outlay of the consumers' goods industries is shifted from fixed to circulating capital. Fixed capital means by definition a large amount of capital per unit of output and the decrease in the demand for fixed capital goods will therefore produce a very much greater decrease of production in the industries producing these capital goods. The simultaneous increase of the demand for circulating capital cannot compensate for this. Because, though the increased demand for circulating capital sets up a positive acceleration effect, this will be much less strong, since much less circulating capital is required per unit of final output. The net result of the initial shift in the outlay of the consumers' goods industries will therefore be a net decrease in the total demand for investment goods—caused ultimately by an excessive increase of final demand.

If this analysis is correct, it is clearly an illusion to expect investment demand to be maintained or revived by keeping up final demand. An increase of final demand may produce this kind of result at the bottom of a depression, when there are large reserves of unused resources in existence. But near the top of a boom it will have the contrary effect: investment will slacken further and it will seem as if there were an absolute lack of investment opportunities, which can be cured only by the government stepping in, while in fact it is the very policy intended to revive private investment which prevents its revival. Again we find that a policy of merely maintaining purchasing power cannot cure unemployment and that those who try to do so will be inevitably driven to control not only the amount of expenditure but also the way in which it is spent.

The worst of the popular illusion, that we can secure full employment by merely securing an adequate supply of expenditure, is, however, not that the hopes that it creates are bound to disappointment, but that it leads to a complete neglect of those measures which really could secure a stable and high level of employment. It will lead us further and further away from a free economy in which reasonable stability can be expected.

('Full Employment Illusions')

23. FULL EMPLOYMENT IN A FREE SOCIETY

In this 1945 review of Full Employment in a Free Society *Professor Hayek highlights two major difficulties with the 'demand-deficiency' analysis of unemployment in the book. Firstly, there are extreme variations in the scale of unemployment from industry to industry and from area to area. These large variations must cast considerable doubt on whether a general lack of demand is the cause of widespread unemployment. Secondly, the book argues that the rise in the marginal propensity to save means that eventually consumer spending must fall short of the value of consumer goods output, thus producing a decline in total output. This argument overlooks the implications of* changes *in output. Since fluctuations in output in the capital goods industries are larger than fluctuations in the consumer goods industries, the marginal propensity to consume tends to be higher than the rate of increase in consumer goods output.*

If the present concern with full employment were the result of a belated recognition of the urgency of the problem, we should have much reason to be ashamed of the past and to congratulate ourselves on the new resolution. But this is not the position.

In England, in particular, unemployment has for nearly a generation been the burning problem that constantly occupied statesmen and economists. The reasons for the intensified agitation must be sought elsewhere. The fact is that the remedies proposed by the economists had been persistently disregarded because they were of a kind that hurt in the application.

Then Lord Keynes assured us that we had all been mistaken and that the cure could be painless and even pleasant: all that was needed to maintain employment permanently at a maximum was to secure an adequate volume of spending of some kind. The argument was not less effective because it was couched in highly technical language. It gave the support of the highest scientific authority to what had always been the popular belief, and the new view gained ground rapidly.

It is the great merit of democracy that the demand for the cure of a widely felt evil can find expression in an organised movement. That popular pressure might become canalised in support of particular theories that sound plausible to the ordinary man is one of its dangers. But it was almost inevitable that some gifted man should see the opportunity and try to ride into political power on the wave of support that could be created for some such scheme. This is what Sir William Beveridge is attempting. His *Full Employment in a Free Society* is as much a political manifesto as a handbook of economic policy. Its appearance coincides with the author's entry into Parliament, and together with his earlier report on social security constitutes his programme of action.

This is not to say that Sir William does not bring special qualifications to the task. But they are not mainly those of the economist. Himself a brilliant expositor who earned his spurs as a leader-writer on one of London's big dailies, a successful administrator with the essential skill of tapping other people's brains, and an acute student of unemployment statistics, he has called in the assistance of a group of younger economists for the more theoretical parts of the book. Its strength and its weakness reflect this origin. The clear exposition and the stress on some important facts that are not always recognised are Sir

William at his best, and the great interest in changes in government machinery equally characteristic.

But the theoretical framework is that of Lord Keynes as seen by his younger disciples and familiar to American readers mainly through the writings of Professor A.H. Hansen. Only one of Sir William's collaborators, N. Kaldor, appears by name as the author of a highly ingenious appendix, which to the economist is the most interesting part of the book and supplies the foundation for much of it.

It is open to question whether the attempt to combine Sir William's characteristic views with the fashionable Keynesian doctrines has made the book more valuable, though it will certainly make it more acceptable to many of the younger economists. Although Sir William is confident that his own approach and 'the revolution of economic thought' effected by J.M. Keynes's are 'not contradictory but complementary', the book leaves many inconsistencies unresolved. One of Sir William's most valuable contributions, e.g., is the emphasis on the extreme diversity of the extent of unemployment from industry to industry and from place to place, which certainly throws much doubt on the adequacy of an explanation in terms of a general deficiency of demand; yet he swallows the demand-deficiency theory lock, stock, and barrel.

Equally important is Sir William's stress on the close connection in Great Britain between unemployment and foreign trade. Yet his remedies are almost entirely of a domestic nature. Indeed, though he realises that hardly any of the imports of Great Britain before the war 'can be described as luxuries', he suggests as a way out 'the alternative of cutting down imports and becoming more independent' because 'the stability of international trade is as important as its scale'. The former champion of free trade has travelled far!

Perhaps most surprising of all is that, while Sir William admits that 'a policy of outlay for full employment, however vigorously it is pursued by the State, will fail to cure unemployment ... if, with peace, industrial demarcations with all the restrictive tendencies and customs of the past return in full force', these factors have no place in his diagnosis of the causes of unemployment. One wonders to what conclusions the author would have been led had they been given their proper place in the analysis and not merely added as an afterthought.

One of the main differences between Sir William's proposals and the British White Paper on employment policy is that Sir William refuses to accept the fact that private investment tends to fluctuate, and to confine himself to compensating measures. As an out-and-out planner, in the modern sense of the term, he proposes to deal with this difficulty by abolishing private investment as we knew it: that is by subjecting all private investment to the direction of a National Investment Board. It is mainly here that apprehensions must arise against which the second half of the title of the book is meant to reassure us. Sir William endeavours to show that, despite all the controls he wishes to impose, 'essential liberties' will be preserved. But private ownership of the means of production is, in his opinion, 'not an essential liberty in Britain, because it is not and never has been enjoyed by more than a very small proportion of the British people'.

It is surprising that he should not yet have learned that private ownership of the means of production is important to most people not because they hope to own such property, but because only such private ownership gives them the choice of competing employers and protects them from being at the mercy of the most complete monopolist ever conceived.

However interesting the points of detail on which Sir William differs from the current Keynes-Hansen theory, much the most important fact about his book is that he lends the weight of his prestige in support of this view. If all the conclusions he draws do not necessarily follow from it, they certainly stand and fall with the belief that a deficiency of final demand is the initial cause of cyclical unemployment.

This theory holds that as employment increases a progressively increasing share of the new income created will not be spent but will be saved. This, it is suggested, must sooner or later produce a situation in which final demand is insufficient to take the output of consumers' goods off the market at remunerative prices. One may grant the first statement and yet deny that the alleged consequences are at all likely to follow. The larger share that is saved out of the additional income would necessarily lead to an insufficiency of final demand only if the additional output contained as large a proportion of consumers' goods as total output.

This assumption seems highly implausible, however. Along with all other students of these matters Sir William stresses that unemployment during a depression is very much greater in the industries making capital goods than in the others. An approach to full employment therefore increases the output of capital goods proportionally much more than the output of consumers' goods. And if no larger proportion of the additional income were saved than was saved out of the smaller income final demand would grow much faster than the supply of consumers' goods.

As a matter of fact, it seems highly unlikely that the share saved out of additional income during a recovery will be even as big as the share of the additional output that is in the form of capital goods. What then becomes of the case that depressions are brought on by over-saving and under-consumption? Of course, we can assume that the decline of investment in a slump *must* be due to an initial deficiency of final demand. This, however, is simply reasoning in a circle.

The cause of the decline of the demand for capital goods must, therefore, be sought elsewhere than in a deficiency of final demand, and may even be an excessive final demand. All the fashionable remedies, including Sir William's, not only fail to touch the root of the matter but may even aggravate the problem. Of course, once final demand shrinks on the scale that will occur as a result of extensive unemployment in the capital goods industries, this will start the vicious spiral of contraction. But the crucial question is: what causes the initial decline of the capital-goods industries?

If, as is more than likely, it is that they tend to overgrow during the boom, all attempts to maintain activity in them at the maximum will only perpetuate the causes of instability.

(Review of Sir William (later Lord) Beveridge's book, *Full Employment in a Free Society*)

Hayek's Writings: A List for Economists

Geldtheorie und Konjunkturtheorie (Vienna and Leipzig: Holder-Pichler-Tempsky, 1929; England, 1933; Japan, 1935; Spain 1936)

Prices and Production (London: Routledge & Kegan Paul, 1931)

Monetary Theory and the Trade Cycle (London: Jonathan Cape, 1933)

Monetary Nationalism and International Stability (Geneva: Universitaire de Hautes Etudes Internationales, 1937)

Profits, Interest and Investment (London: Routledge & Kegan Paul, 1939)

The Pure Theory of Capital (London: Routledge & Kegan Paul, 1941)

The Road to Serfdom (London: Routledge & Kegan Paul, 1944)

Individualism and Economic Order (London and Chicago: University of Chicago Press, 1948; Germany 1952)

John Stuart Mill and Harriet Taylor (London and Chicago: University of Chicago Press, 1951

The Sensory Order (London: Routledge & Kegan Paul, 1952)

The Counter-Revolution of Science (Glencoe, Ill.: The Free Press, 1955)

The Political Ideal of the Rule of Law (Cairo: National Bank of Egypt, 1955)

The Constitution of Liberty (London: Routledge & Kegan Paul, 1960)

Studies in Philosophy, Politics and Economics (London: Routledge & Kegan Paul, 1967)

Law, Legislation and Liberty, 3 vols. (London: Routledge & Kegan Paul): Vol. 1: *Rules and Order* (1973); Vol. II: *The Mirage of Social Justice* (1976); Vol. III: *The Political Order of a Free Society* (1979)

New Studies in Philosophy, Politics, Economics and the History of Ideas (London: Routledge & Kegan Paul, 1978)

Index

Age of Keynes, The, 3n
Angewandte Lohntheorie, 78n
Arbeiterfrage unter dem Gesichtspunkte des Vereinsrechtes, Die, 74n

Balogh, T., 6
Bamberger, Ludwig, 74n
Bank for International Settlements, 50
Barnard, C.I., 88n
Bernanke, Ben, xv
Beveridge, Lord, 6, 152–53
Böhm-Bawerk, Eugen von, 9
Böhm, Franz, 90n
Bradley, P.D., 78n
Briefs, Goetz, 90n
Britain's Economic Prospects, 6n
Brittan, S., 6, 7

Capital. *See* Investment
Capitalism, Socialism, and Democracy, 75n
Caves, R.E., 6n
Chamberlin, E.H., 76n, 78n, 87n
Clark, J.M., 2
Clearing Union, 44, 51, 54
Clower, R.W., 9n
Cole, G.D.H., xii
Commodity Reserve Currency, 41–43, 43–47, 47–55, 56–57

Constitution of Liberty, 101, 110
Critics of Keynesian Economics, The, 4n

Davenport, John, 78n
Deflation, 24, 101–110
Depression, xiv, xvi–xvii, xix
Dicey, A.C., 75n,
Dunlop, J.T., 77n, 78n

Economic Analysis of Labor Power, 78n
Economic Growth in Britain, 6n
Economic Institute on Wage Determination and the
Economics of Liberalism, 77n
Economist in the Century, The, 6n
Economists and the Public, 4n, 77n
Employment, 12, 73–76, 144
  full, 2–7, 59–67, 115–17, 124, 139, 143
  unemployment, xii, xiv, 3, 5, 47, 53–54, 59, 66, 139, 145, 151–56
    cyclical, 146–47, 154
    parallel with monopoly, 141
    as wage problem, 140
    White Paper, 1944, 2, 154

Federal Reserve, xv
Fellner, William, 14n

Fisher, Irving, 24, 44
Freedom under Planning, 98n
Full Employment in a Free Society, 151–56

Gascom, Charles, xivn
Gemeinwirtschaft, Die, 76n
General Theory of Employment, Interest and Money, passim
Gold Standard, 41–43, 43–46, 50–51, 114
Gouldner, A.W., 89n
Government
   bailout, xiv, xix
   Stimulus program, xiii
Government and the Market Economy, 6n, 7n
Graham, F.D.
   criticises Keynes, 47
   Keynes replies to Graham, 56

Hansen, A.H., 153, 154
Hayek, F.A., passim
   criticises Keynes, 12–13, 30–31, 111
   criticised by Keynes, 43
Hazlitt, Henry, 4n
Hicks, J.R., 78n, 95n
How to pay for the War, 4
Hunold, A., 105n
Hutt, W.H., xxi, 4, 4n, 77n

Impact of the Union, The, 78n
Incomes Policy, 5, 8, 13–14, 45, 55, 96–99
Individualism and Economic Order, 10n, 14n
Industrial Democracy, 89
Industrial Relations in Australia, 98n
Industry and Society, 88n
Industry-wide Bargaining, 78n
Inflation, xviii, 15–24, 59–67, 101–10, 115–17, 129–34, 135–38
   cause, 4, 67–73, 95, 132–34, 145
   cost push, 5–8, 23–24, 94–96
   demand pull, 5n, 9
   German, 144

   international, 20–21
   monetary, xv, xix
Investment, 6–9, 12, 27–30, 34–37, 114–15, 146–47, 150, 155
   abolish private investment, 154
Involuntary Participation in Unionism, 78

Johnson, H.J., 10n

Kaldor, N., 3, 154
Keynes, J.M., passim
   criticised by Hayek, 12–13, 30–31, 111
   criticises Hayek, 43
   criticised by Graham, 47
   reply to Graham, 56–57
   The Critics of Keynesian Economics, 4n
   reatise on Money, xxii, 12, 112
Keynesianism, xvi

Labor Policy of the Free Society, The, 78n, 93
Labour,
   employment, xiv, xvi, 2, 3, 139
   employment White Paper (1944), 3, 154
   immobility, 141
   movement, 63–65
   strike, 78, 91
   unemployment, xiv, xviii, 2–4, 46, 53–55, 61–65, 80, 93–96, 127, 142
   unionized, xvii
Labour and Inflation, 6n
Labour Unions and Public Policy, 76n
Law and Opinion, 75n
Legal Immunities of Labour Unions, 76n
Lekachman, Robert, 3n
Lenhoff, A, 93n
Lindblom, C.B., 78n
Lutz, F., 14n, 105n

Machlup, F., 5n, 78n
Marshall, A., 1, 113
Marx, Karl, 48

INDEX

McCulloch, J.R., 74n
McDermott, Lord, 76n
Meade, James, 6
Menger, Carl, 9
Mill, John Stuart, 125
Mills, C.W., 74n
Mises, L. von, 9, 76n, 113, 137
Monetary Policy, xv, 8–13, 16–17, 24–25, 37–39, 60–67, 120–25, 138, 140–41
   exchange rates, 22–24, 45–46, 50–53
   interest rate, 29–30, 33, 37,
   reforms, 7, 11, 41–44, 46, 47
   reserve currency, 41–57
Monetary Nationalism and International Stability, 17, 24, 25
Monetary Theory, 10n
Money
   quantity, 20–22, 31, 44, 107, 113, 136, 143–44
   stock, 10, 16, 45–46, 72
   supply, xxn
Monopoly
   capitalist, 141, 145
   labour, 141, 145
   parallel with unemployment, 141
Morgan, E.V., 6, 7

National Investment Board, 154
New Men of Power, The, 74n
Norris-La Guardia Act, 76

Obama, Barack (President), xv
Ohlin, B, 24n
Opie, R, 6
Organization and Management, 88n

Paish, Frank, 6, 7
Patterns of Industrial Bureaucracy, 89n
Petro, Sylvester, 77n, 78n, 88n, 93, 99
Pigou, A.C., xxii, 1, 113
Planning, 59, 60, 96–99, 110, 127, 130, 145
Political Economy of Monopoly, The, 78n
Pound, Roscoe, 78n

Power Unlimited: The Corruption of Union Leadership, 77n
Price Level
   fallacy of, 17–24
Prices. *See* Inflation
Prices and Production, 10, 12, 15, 17, 112
Problem of Rising Prices, The, 14n
Production, 10–13, 16–16, 34–35, 115, 136, 145–50, 154
   costs of, xvii
   factors of, 31–33
Profit, 12, 33, 37, 69
   margins, 102–04, 148
   sharing, 132
Protection from Power under English Law, 76n
Pure Theory of Capital, The, 37, 40

Real factors
   importance of, xvii, 34–37
   scarcity of, xvii, xviii, 27–33
Recession, xiii
Reddaway. W.B., 8n
Reilly, G.D., 8n
Rise and Fall of Incomes Policy, 6n
Robbins, Lord, 6, 6n
Roberts, B.C., 78n
Robertson, D.H., xxii
Robertson, D.J., 6n
Roepke, W., 102n
Rubber, 21

Saving, 12, 34–37, 154–56
Schumpeter, J.A., 75n
Sherman Act, 76
Short run
   dangers of, 37–40
Simons, H.C., 77n
Slichter, Sumner, 89n
Smith, Adam, xxi
Smith, D.C., 6n
Smithies, Arthur, 2, 2n
Sobotka, S.P., 83n
South Africa, 48

Stabilization policy, xvi
Stagflation, 143
State Rights and the Law of Labor Relations, 78n
Streeten, P.P., 5, 5n
Strigi, R., 78n
Studies in Philosophy, Politics, and Economics, 14n, 67

Theory of Collective Bargaining, 4n, 77n
Theory of Idle Resources, 4n
Theory of Money, 113
Theory of Wage Determination, The, 78n
Theory of Wages, The, 78n
'Tiger by the Tail,' 13, 125
Trade International, 65, 114, 153
Trade Unions, 73–101, 125
    coercion, 77–101
    monopoly, 73, 83
    strike, right to, 78, 90–91
    wage demands, 4, 7, 9, 13–14, 67–73, 73–85, 95–96
Trade Unions in a Free Society, 78n, 89n
Treatise on the Circumstances Which Determine the Rate of Wages and the Condition of the Labouring Classes, 74n
Treatise on Money, xxii, 12, 112
Two Memoirs, 118

Unions and Capitalism, 78n, 80n
Uri, P., 3

Viner, Jacob, 3, 3n, 78n
Vollbeschäftigung, Inflation und Planwirtschaft, 105n

Wage Determination under Trade Unions, 77n
Wages, 1–9, 13–14, 17–19, 44–46, 59–60, 119–125, 140–41, 144–45
    bargaining, 24, 78
    incomes Policy, 5, 6, 7, 13, 45, 55, 96–99
    inflexibility, 59–110
    reduction, 23, 25, 67–70, 94–96, 127
Wages and Prices in a Mixed Economy, 6n
Walker, E.R., 3
Walker, K.F., 3
War financing, 4
Weintraub, S., 98n
Welfare, Freedom, and Inflation, 102n
What Marx Really Meant, xxii
Wieser, F. von, 9
Whyte, W.F., 88n
Williams Gertrud, 98n
Wolman, Leo, 78n
Wootton, Barbara, 77n, 98n
Wright, David McCord, 78n

Zwischen Kapitalismus und Syndikalismus, 90n

LargePrintLiberty.com

Dedicated to offering books on libertarian thought and economics in Large Print paperback.

Titles include:

For a New Liberty, by Murray N. Rothbard (Philosophy)
"A classic that for over two decades has been hailed as the best general work on libertarianism available. Rothbard begins with a quick overview of its historical roots, and then goes on to define libertarianism as resting 'upon one single axiom: that no man or group of men shall aggress upon the person or property of anyone else.' He writes a withering critique of the chief violator of liberty: the State. Rothbard then provides penetrating libertarian solutions for many of today's most pressing problems, including poverty, war, threats to civil liberties, the education crisis, and more."

Principles of Economics, by Carl Menger (Economics)
"In the beginning, there was Menger. It was this book that reformulated, and really rescued, economic science. It kicked off the Marginalist Revolution, which corrected theoretical errors of the old classical school. These errors concerned value theory, and they had sown enough confusion to make the dangerous ideology of Marxism seem more plausible than it really was. Menger set out to elucidate the precise nature of economic value, and root economics firmly in the real-world actions of individual human beings."

Great Wars and Great Leaders, by Ralph Raico (History)
"In the backdrop of this blistering and deeply insightful and scholarly history is the whitewashing of 'great leaders' like Woodrow Wilson, Winston Churchill, FDR, Truman, Stalin, Trotsky, and other collectivists. They are highly regarded because they were on the 'right side' of the rise of the state. But do they deserve adulation? Raico says no: these great leaders were main agents in the decline of civilization in the 20th century, all of them anti-liberals who used their power to celebrate and enhance state power."

www.ingramcontent.com/pod-product-compliance
Lightning Source LLC
Chambersburg PA
CBHW080244180526
45167CB00006B/2409